CONTEMPORARY ISSUES

FAIR TRADE AND HOW IT WORKS

JACQUELINE DECARLO

ROSEN PUBLISHING®

New York

This edition published in 2011 by:

The Rosen Publishing Group, Inc.
29 East 21st Street
New York, NY 10010

Additional end matter copyright © 2011 by The Rosen Publishing Group, Inc.

Library of Congress Cataloging-in-Publication Data

DeCarlo, Jacqueline.
Fair trade and how it works / Jacqueline DeCarlo.
    p. cm.—(Contemporary issues)
Includes bibliographical references and index.
ISBN 978-1-4488-1865-5 (library binding)
1. International trade—Moral and ethical aspects—Juvenile literature. 2. Competition, Unfair—Juvenile literature. 3. Social responsibility of business—Juvenile literature. 4. Developing countries—Commerce—Juvenile literature. I. Title.
HF1379.D43 2011
382'.3—dc22

                                                                        2010029795

Manufactured in the United States of America

CPSIA Compliance Information: Batch #W11YA: For further information, contact Rosen Publishing, New York, New York, at 1-800-237-9932.

Originally published in 2007 as part of the Oneworld Beginner's Guides series. Copyrigth © Jacqueline DeCarlo 2007

Contents

Acknowledgements

I believe that Fair Trade improves lives because it has improved mine. For the past seven years, I have been privileged to meet with and learn from Fair Traders around the globe who have shaped my understanding of and commitment to Fair Trade principles and practices. Many of them helped in the writing of this book, and it would be foolish to try and name them all. I sincerely hope that the people who have participated in my research, who have collaborated with me at the Fair Trade Resource Network and Catholic Relief Services, and who have challenged me along different paths to economic justice will take credit for the role they have played. I owe a large intellectual and emotional debt to participants in the Fair Trade Futures conference.

I am also grateful to my circle of friends and family who have accompanied me through various parts of my Fair Trade journey. I treasure each of you. I especially thank Kathy E. McKee for her steadfast faith in my abilities since our first semester of college and Kristen Leslie Moe for her companionship and support. I thank my mother for her support in all areas of my life, even when she was not sure what I was up to. I hope this book makes my travels and choices easier to understand.

My greatest hope is that this book serves in some measure to honor artisans and farmers and to advance their aspirations for lives of dignity and opportunity in partnership with conscious consumers and advocates. I am grateful to the team at Oneworld Publications for the opportunity to create this resource together.

Illustrations, tables, and key boxes

1

Fair Trade: why it's not just for coffee farmers anymore

Overview: as we embark on our exploration of Fair Trade, this chapter considers the context for Fair Trade at the global, societal, and personal levels. A definition of Fair Trade is supplied and a roadmap to the rest of the guide is presented.

Generally speaking, residents of the United States, like myself, do not think of Canadians as a rowdy bunch. They are, according to benign stereotypes, our kinder, gentler neighbors to the north, not known for making a ruckus, unless watching a contentious hockey game. So, I was delighted one September evening in 2005 to witness a dozen Canadian fair traders, proudly waving a banner of the International Fair Trade Association (I.F.A.T.) and chanting, "Hey, hey, ho, ho: Fair Trade is the way to go." These Canadians were not, I should say from the outset, at an antiglobalization demonstration in front of the World Bank or International Monetary Fund. They were crowded into a Chicago, Illinois, hotel banquet hall with some 750 consumers, producers, businesses, and advocates from twenty countries to partake in the first Fair Trade Futures conference.

I start this beginner's guide with a reference to the conference, not only because the event was a testament to the vitality and credibility of the phenomenon known as Fair Trade, but because each attendee was, most probably, similar to the typical reader of a beginner's guide. Each individual came to the conference with a common desire to understand what Fair Trade is about and how, or whether, she or he wanted to "Live a Fair Trade Life," as the conference motto suggested. I imagine a beginner's guide reader to be the kind of person who is drawn to the notion of Fair Trade for a variety of reasons.

Maybe she's traveled to other countries and knows firsthand about the incredible poverty that billions of people struggle with

1

on a daily basis. She has heard that Fair Trade helps create income for poor people.

Maybe his place of worship promotes Fair Trade, but he's never had a chance to read the congregation newsletter as to why. Now this reader is willing to spend a bit of time to dig deeper to find out if Fair Trade matches his values.

Maybe the reader is a college student who has never joined a campus campaign but has heard a lot of buzz about Fair Trade in the dining hall. Maybe she can even earn some extra credits for reading this book.

Maybe he is an American curious about a little black-and-white label that keeps popping up at the grocery store or a European seeking information about what the blue-and-green seal in the supermarket means.

Maybe she is a business leader who cares about workers and customers. This reader wants to know what this latest trend in social responsibility is all about.

If any of these matches your profile or interests, Fair Trade may be for you. It is definitely for billions of people in isolated villages and dilapidated shantytowns who haven't experienced all the benefits of globalization or "free trade." Fair Trade is for regular women and men who

FAIR TRADE DEFINITION

Fair Trade is a trading partnership, based on dialogue, transparency, and respect, that seeks greater equity in international trade. It contributes to sustainable development by offering better trading conditions to, and securing the rights of, marginalized producers and workers – especially in the South. Fair Trade Organizations (backed by consumers) are actively engaged in supporting producers, in awareness raising and in campaigning for changes in the rules and practices of conventional international trade.

Endorsed by F.I.N.E., a group composed of the Fairtrade Labeling Organizations International, the International Fair Trade Association, the Network of European Worldshops, and the European Fair Trade Association.

want to work hard, play by fair rules, and take advantage of sustainable economic opportunities, yet find few options available to them. It is particularly for undereducated women and other disadvantaged groups fighting to survive on the fringes of society in the face of discrimination or against invisibility in a world where the rich and powerful are held up as role models.

My goal for this guide is to help the reader understand and analyze Fair Trade. I want this because I believe that Fair Trade is one solution to poverty and marginalization. I also believe it can address some of the problems consumers face in what is now commonly called the Global North, the set of industrialized countries that have relatively robust economies and stable governments. Overconsumption, unethical business practices, and environmental concerns can all be observed through the lens of Fair Trade. All around the globe, Fair Trade has the potential to reshape how products are made and consumed. As such, it can influence how we relate to each other as human beings.

Right now in many places and in many ways, relations are not all that encouraging. Of greatest concern to me is the gap between rich and poor people and nations. The United Nations estimates that a person needs at least four dollars a day, about $1500 a year, to live a basic, decent life. By this measure, of the 6.5 billion people in the world today, four billion people do not live a decent life. Of those, fully one billion live on less than one dollar a day. Yet, at the same moment in history, at least seventy-five million people have *at least* fifty-five dollars worth of purchasing power a day. In the United States, 300 million people, roughly four percent of the world's population, consume more than twenty-five percent of the planet's energy resources. Meanwhile, the four billion impoverished people live in rural villages, or urban slums and shantytowns, where they have limited access to social services such as health care, education, water, electricity and transportation.

Readers may have encountered these statistics before. I am not going to make the familiar argument that this level of consumption is unsustainable. I am not going to deconstruct history and blame inequality on colonialism or corruption or even capitalism. I am merely going to point out what you probably already suspect: this type of disparity is not acceptable. This beginner's guide will help explore whether Fair Trade can help change the way the world works for all of us on the planet.

Figure 1 Women in Africa and around the world find opportunity through Fair Trade.

Consumers definitely benefit from Fair Trade. They obtain unique, high-quality products. But more than that, they are involved in a powerful type of consumption. Through this guide you can consider the impact and influence of your purchases and how they connect you with people in your own community and country and around the world. As is often said, a dollar – or a pound or a Euro – is an economic ballot. Consumers make choices each and every day about how to spend money and exercise economic power. What clothes to buy, what Internet service provider to use, what cars to drive, what food to buy. When consumers make conscious decisions about how to spend money on items that do not depend on the exploitation of human labor, the destruction of the environment, or the homogenization of culture, they are voting for the kind of world they want to live in. And, they are engaged in creating that world. The topic of free trade will come up in this beginner's guide, and I argue that a frequently overlooked freedom of our current trading system comes from being able to exert individual power – economic, political, and moral – to support Fair Trade.

But consumers cannot do this alone. The immense problems of poverty cannot be solved by Fair Trade by itself. Development assistance, improved governance structures, and even reformed conventional trade in the sectors that Fair Trade does not involve, such as technology and transportation, are all parts of a multifaceted solution to poverty and lack of opportunity. At the turn of this century, the United Nations (U.N.) adopted a set of goals and targets for combating poverty, hunger, disease, illiteracy, environmental degradation, and discrimination against women. These are referred to as the Millennium Development Goals, and they provide the entire U.N. system with a framework for reaching them by 2015. Former Secretary General Kofi Annan has said:

> We will have time to reach the Millennium Development Goals – worldwide and in most, or even all, individual countries – but only if we break with business as usual. We cannot win overnight. Success will require sustained action across the entire decade between now and the deadline. It takes time to train the teachers, nurses, and engineers; to build the roads, schools and hospitals; to grow the small and large businesses able to create the jobs and income needed.

In this guide, I share some of my personal and professional influences, as well as insights and analysis from producers and consumers with whom I am fortunate to be connected by virtue of the shared concerns and aspirations referred to as Fair Trade. Despite my use of the term "Fair Trade" as if it were a monolith, we will see early into our exploration that Fair Trade encompasses a diverse array of interpretations and manifestations. All over the world ardent fair traders are debating and refining what Fair Trade is and is not. Still, I have consciously used the term movement to describe this phenomenon. This designation in part reflects my aspirations that Fair Trade will become a force that transforms society alongside labor and solidarity movements, civil rights movements, and peace and justice movements.

THE MILLENNIUM DEVELOPMENT GOALS
TO BE ACHIEVED BY 2015

End Poverty and Hunger: Reduce by half the proportion of people living on less than $1 a day. Reduce by half the proportion of people who suffer from hunger.

Education for All: Ensure children everywhere, boys and girls alike, will be able to complete a full course of primary schooling.

Equality for Women: Eliminate gender disparity in education.

Save Children's Lives: Reduce by two-thirds the under-five mortality rate.

Make Motherhood Safe: Reduce the maternal mortality ratio by three-quarters.

Stop HIV/AIDS, Malaria, and Other Diseases: Have halted and begun to reverse the spread of HIV/AIDS. Have halted and begun to reverse the incidence of malaria and other major diseases.

Protect the Environment: Integrate the principles of sustainable development into country policies and programs, and reverse the loss of environmental resources. Reduce by half the proportion of people without sustainable access to safe drinking water and basic sanitation. Achieve significant improvement in the lives of at least 100 million slum dwellers by 2020.

Build a Global Partnership for Development: Address needs of the least developed countries. Further develop an open trading and financial system. Deal comprehensively with developing countries' debt. Develop job strategies for youth. Provide access to affordable essential drugs in developing countries. Make available new technologies, especially information and communications.

Especially here, in my home country of the United States, I want Fair Trade to affect fundamental change in the way Americans think about their consumption, their relationships to others, and their place in the world. But, I recognize that Fair Trade is many things to many people. "Movement" may be too broad a term, and "business model" definitely too narrow. Some, such as Fair Trade pioneer Pauline Tiffen, suggest thinking of Fair Trade as being part of a "marketplace," a more humane and spirited collection of activities than the neutral, invisible market of economist Adam Smith. And we can go even further, as human beings are more than consumers in the marketplace. We must pay attention to the real benefits and costs of purchases, but our biggest concern as fair traders may be the awareness that the best things in life are not things we can buy.

I stopped in my tracks during a morning jog in Washington, D.C., recently when I saw an advertisement for a luxury car that read, "A strong want is a justifiable need." I reject the notion advertisers relentlessly promote: that consumers are entitled to everything they want, or everything marketers want them to want. Through Fair Trade, consumers can help themselves and others meet their basic and sustainable needs. With Fair Trade modern consumers can rethink some of the entrenched attitudes of our generation.

In many ways, my philosophical approach to the many meanings of Fair Trade is not new. In chapter two I consider the roles the free market economy plays in our lives and in relation to Fair Trade. Chapters three and four examine the principles of Fair Trade and how they are linked to fine traditions of justice embodied by outstanding individuals and enterprises. I describe in chapter five the rather humble beginnings of Fair Trade, rooted in people-to-people partnerships, and the array of organizations at the forefront of its development. Chapter six considers whether and how Fair Trade affects lives, and in chapter seven, I offer the examples of average people who make those impacts possible. Chapter eight will help put Fair Trade in the broader political context of the international trading system.

At this point, I offer another clarification about terminology: the first time the term "Fair Trade" was used in its current context was by author and advocate Michael Barratt Brown at a conference in London. Up to that point in the movement, the term "alternative trade" had been used. The word "alternative" reflected nontraditional methods to reach markets such as craft sales in church basements. It suggested a different way to do business that favored the marginalized and disadvantaged and it strove for alternative mechanisms to reform an international trade system that Oxfam has since dubbed as being full of "rigged rules and double standards." Barratt Brown distilled those goals into the desire for "fairness." However, as the Fair Trade movement evolves, some consider the current usage of Fair Trade too limited in that it can be narrowed in application to only a fair price. Others find it inferior to goals such as those of the solidarity trade movement, which seeks to nurture local, community-based markets. The future of Fair Trade, which is the consideration of chapter nine, will be shaped by how consumers interpret these debates. Chapter ten closes the guide with ideas for how the reader can broaden Fair Trade commitments and participate in defining the future. I also offer an appendix and list of readings for deeper exploration because this book is more than a guide, it is an invitation to take a role in shaping what the future of Fair Trade can be.

2

Fish don't know they are wet *or* how trading influences our lives

Overview: this chapter orients us to the consideration of Fair Trade by locating it within the context and systems of our daily lives. We consider our daily participation in the market to compare conventional trade to the Fair Trade model.

When I speak to secondary school classes about Fair Trade in my role as a Fair Trade educator, I often begin by asking one of the teenagers if I can borrow a pen for the lesson. Once I have it in my hands, I extravagantly praise the pen, noting its cool colors and its sleek design. Then I offer to purchase it from the student. More often than not, the student says I can "just keep it." I pretend to be astonished by her suggestion and say, "Well, can I have your book bag too?" The student looks at me skeptically and shakes her head "no." Undeterred I ask, "Okay, but I really like it. Can I buy it from you?" At this point, other students jump in, some offering their own bags for sale. I proceed with some mock negotiations and begin to take the exercise into a discussion of why things in our life have a price, teasing out the notions of value and cost. I end up with neither a new book bag nor a pen in my possession, but a solid platform for a discussion of Fair Trade.

This beginner's guide needs a similar platform, so let's start with the object in your hands: the book itself. How did you come by this book? Was it a gift? Was it borrowed from the public library? Did you buy it in a bookstore or online? In any of these cases, a price was paid for the book. That price was based on a variety of factors, including costs for the author's time, the editor's skill, the talents of the graphic designer, the quality of the paper, and so on. Consideration was also taken as to what price a potential reader was willing to pay or, as the economists say, "what the market will bear."

A beginner's guide reader is an example of the modern-day consumer in the Global North: an individual who interacts with the market on a daily basis in a variety of ways, many of which seem automatic or natural. Consumers want and need books, pens, and a whole range of other goods and services. They work jobs or earn an allowance to accumulate money, which they then exchange to satisfy wants and needs. None of this probably strikes the reader as being anything but normal. Like the proverbial fish in a pond that doesn't realize it is wet, consumers don't usually think of the methods of exchange they use to trade labor for cash or cash for dinner or a new pair of shoes. Nor are they necessarily aware of the variety of intra-governmental structures, such as the World Trade Organization, that set the terms and facilitate the functioning of trade.

Yet, it is important to understand, at least at a rudimentary level, how economic exchange takes place in order to understand how Fair Trade principles play out and why Fair Trade is a distinct alternative to the "business as usual" model of conventional trade. Let's consider a little more carefully the typical supply, or value, chain of Fair Trade. A value chain describes the production, marketing, and delivery links required for a commodity, product, or service to arrive from a producer to a customer. In our globalized economy, the links very often spread across countries, economies, and institutions. Transactions between and among links create economic and social relationships. The question becomes: what types of relationships? Those that foster partnerships, as in the Fair Trade model, or those where shareholder profit motives predominate?

The diagram offered by Café Campesino, coffee roasters offering Fair Trade, organically grown coffee, illustrates key elements in the Fair Trade path, or chain, for coffee. The chain starts with the farmer who plants, cultivates, harvests, and processes the coffee beans. He or she sells those beans to an association, or cooperative, that is responsible for representing the farmer's interests with financiers and buyers in order to access coffee markets. The buyers package, roast, and market the coffee, either through wholesale or retail mechanisms, to customers.

Many times proponents of Fair Trade will say that the model eliminates the middleman, but as we see with coffee, that's not technically the case. The farmer sells to a cooperative. Lenders provide credit to ensure working capital for the cooperative. Roasters buy from importers who purchased the beans. Retailers buy the beans to sell to consumers. There are links – middlemen – in the coffee supply chain. Unless we

Table 1. Campesino coffee chain

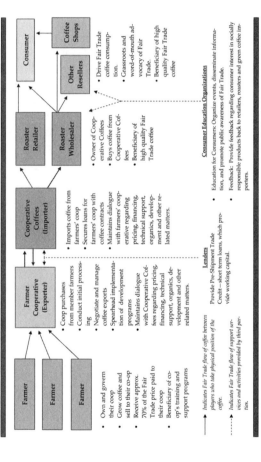

Critical Steps along the Fair Trade Coffee Path*
from crop to cup . . . a fair trade

Farmer

Farmer

Farmer

- Own and govern their coop
- Grow coffee and sell to their co-op
- Receive approx. 70% of the Fair Trade price paid to their coop
- Beneficiary of co-op's training and support programs

Farmer Cooperative (Exporter)

- Coop purchases from member farmers
- Conduct initial processing
- Negotiate and manage coffee exports
- Spearhead implementation of development programs
- Maintains dialogue with Cooperative Coffees regarding pricing, financing, technical support, organics, development and other related matters.

Cooperative Coffees (Importer)

- Imports coffee from farmers' coop
- Secures loans for coffee contracts
- Maintains dialogue with farmers' cooperative regarding pricing, financing, technical support, organics, development and other related matters.

Roaster Retailer

Roaster Wholesaler

- Owner of Cooperative Coffees
- Buys coffee from Cooperative Coffees
- Beneficiary of high quality Fair Trade coffee

Consumer

Coffee Shops

Other Resellers

- Drive Fair Trade coffee consumption.
- Grassroots and word-of-mouth advocacy of Fair Trade.
- Beneficiary of high quality Fair Trade coffee

→ *Indicates Fair Trade flow of coffee between players who take physical position of the coffee.*

- - → *Indicates Fair Trade flow of support services and activities provided by third parties.*

Lenders
Provide Pre-Shipment Trade Credit—short term loans, which provide working capital.

Consumer Education Organizations

- Education for Consumers: Organize events, disseminate information, and promote public awareness of Fair Trade.
- Feedback: Provide feedback regarding consumer interest in socially responsible products back to retailers, roasters and green coffee importers.

Café Campesino • 888-532-4728 • www.cafecampesino.com • Americus, GA

* Graphics adapted from the "Fair Trade Value Chain" by Ecologic Finance.

grow and produce every single product that we use and consume in our lives, there will always be intermediaries who get products and services to the marketplace. The supply chain is necessary and can be extremely beneficial if the transactions are conducted in a principled manner with as much value kept by the producer as possible. All too often, however, desperately poor people whose communities lack infrastructure, such as paved roads, or whose families lack transportation, such as trucks, are at the mercy of middlemen, who take advantage of their desperation to buy crops or products at very low prices. Along the chain, too, can be middlemen who demand excessive profit margins for the services that they are providing, like transportation. This price gouging increases costs along the chain, effectively reducing the value that could stay with producers.

In his influential book, *Fair Trade: Reform and Realities in the International Trading System*, Michael Barratt Brown identifies no less than eighteen links in a typical commodity chain. He also makes a compelling case for how dominant multinational corporations exert inordinate power along the chain, particularly in the realms of shipping and access to credit. The heart of the matter, says Brown, is that a small number of giant companies derive power, "from the scale of their resources, the integration of their operations ... their access to finance ... and increasingly the freedom they enjoy to switch supplies from one source to another, and even to switch operations from plantations to outgrowing."

Fair Trade seeks to remove exploitative middlemen and to establish roles that provide producers the means and mechanisms to exert more power and receive more equitable portions of value. In fact, I prefer the term "value chain" to "supply chain" to convey the fact that each transaction holds the potential to transfer value between parties. Fair Trade researcher Laura Raynolds also suggests that traditional analysis of supply chains is limited because the network of relationships involved in the consumer end of the chain is overlooked. Values concerning price, quality, and politics are also transmitted along the value chain.

Returning to the high school students interested in Fair Trade, I note that the value they ascribe to a book bag often goes beyond its actual functionality into the realm of popular styles and color trends. These things add value for the teenagers involved because students associate book bags and other accessories with acceptance and popularity among peers. For fair traders, there is explicit, monetary value along the supply chain, *and*, as Raynolds suggests, there is a network of relationships that can be constructed and nurtured through Fair Trade that conveys less tangible but no less potent values.

Differences between Fair Trade and free trade

The Reverend Doctor Martin Luther King Jr. famously noted that by the time we finish eating breakfast, we have relied on half of the world. Well before the recent surge of free trade agreements and even the Internet-powered era of globalization, Dr. King was trying to help consumers see that we are benefiting from global networks of human and natural resources. As I sit typing this chapter, I use a laptop whose components were manufactured in Taiwan but assembled in San Francisco. Via the Internet, I can do research on fair traders in Asia or Africa. As I bundle up in a chilly apartment, I wear a shirt that was made in Venezuela and a sweater made in Hong Kong. Earlier I had dinner at a restaurant that served locally grown organic lettuce on a plate with rice from India and tilapia from Latin America. I have access to all these products and services because of the power and reach of what is commonly called a free market economy.

Yet the United Nations reports that one-quarter of the world's population lives on less than two dollars a day. Two billion human beings have no access to electricity, and more than one billion people have no access to clean water. It becomes clear that globalization is not working for everyone. Vast inequalities exist between me, a middle-class North American, and the farmers, factory workers, and craftspeople around the world who make my lifestyle possible. Classic liberal economist Martin Wolf acknowledges as much but argues in his book, *Why Globalization Works*, that "to bemoan ... increase in inequality [as a result of dynamic growth] is to bemoan the growth itself. It is to argue that it would be better for everybody to be equally poor than for some to become significantly better off, even if, in the long run, this will almost certainly lead to advances for everybody." He goes on to say, "The soaring growth of the rapidly integrating developing economies has transformed the world for the better. The challenge is to bring those who have failed so far into the new web of productive and profitable global economic relations."

Fair Trade is a significant and useful way to bring producers in developing countries into productive and profitable relations. It is also, unlike conventional trade, a way to infuse those relations with the principles defined at the beginning of this book. Although it is true that multinational corporations provide jobs and investments in developing countries, the standard model of setting up a factory in a country and giving local people the "opportunity" to work there often falls quite short of Fair Trade principles. In 2004, I met with women in the community of Santa Cruz, Brazil, who had been hired to work in a clothing factory. The women got paid, although they had no say over what their wages were. None of the women I met, though, complained to me about the wages. It was their spirits that were lacking.

They found the work deeply unsatisfying because the monotonous machinery created the same product over and over again. Working at the factory as seamstresses didn't allow them to practice their traditional sewing techniques. These are women who have a reputation for making sequined costumes for *Carnaval*. They were also known for creating patchwork bedspreads. But that's not what they were producing in this new factory. And the women, although grateful for the jobs, felt diminished by the lack of control over their destinies. They felt that although they desperately needed the factory income, they were in danger of losing their community's sewing heritage and their self-expression. They used up all their time and energy working for the factory.

A woman I only know as Rosemary decided to organize a sewing cooperative that preserved the seamstress tradition, gave women the right to determine their own prices, and provided afterschool care for the children of the members. The women had begun to worry about their children, who had to stay at home alone after school, in poor, sometimes dangerous neighborhoods. This cooperative, Cooperativa de Costura, is an example of Fair Trade in contrast to conventional trade. Cooperative members are designing and creating their own products, are setting their own prices to work their way out of poverty, and are protecting their children.

This work environment and the control over one's own destiny are in sharp contrast to the sweatshop abuses discovered by groups, such as the National Labor Committee (N.L.C.). A May 2006 report by N.L.C. revealed that guest workers in Jordan were being forced to work 109 hours a week, and if they fell asleep, they were struck with a ruler to rouse them. Although I do not want to suggest that all factories are sweatshops, in the free market system bottom-line concerns over how much profit is earned or how much shareholder wealth is gained dictate business strategies. Concerns about worker empowerment or decision making are not central to conventional trade. Furthermore, as Pauline Tiffen, former director of Twin Trading and cofounder of the Day Chocolate Company, has pointed out, "Take almost any mainstream branded product now and unfortunately behind it is a tale of merger, acquisition, brand hegemony, theft of intellectual property and assets, exploitation of natural resources, and market concentration." We have focused on worker well-being but conventional trade is equally guilty of environmental exploitation, key examples being the extractive industries such as oil and diamonds. In contrast, Fair Trade – while concerned with economic viability – does not focus on a profit motive at the expense of producers and the environment.

Fair Trade puts disadvantaged, economically poor people at the center of its concern. In an era of "socially responsible" businesses, this distinction is critical. There are many enlightened entrepreneurs, such as Yvon Chouinard of Patagonia or Jeffrey Hollender of Seventh Generation who have demonstrated that it is possible to do well by doing good. These business models should be applauded and supported. But they are not, strictly speaking, Fair Trade. The distinction is important in a progressive sense because these businesses can look to Fair Trade for possible standards and strategies to emulate. But the distinction also has a negative potential because there are a range of ways to align a business with Fair Trade without necessarily making fundamental commitments to its principles. Moreover, there are businesses that seek to distract consumers from disreputable practices with corporate philanthropy or outright deception. In this climate, fair traders can be distinguished through their consistent focus on the empowerment of the economically disadvantaged. Carol Wills, immediate past executive director of I.F.A.T., current chair of the British Association of Fair Trade Shops, and a non-executive director of Shared Interest, explains the priorities of fair traders:

> Fair Traders began their work with handicrafts as a means of supporting very poor people, especially women, to trade their way out of poverty. Handicraft producers tend to live on or below the poverty line. They

are often landless and have few skills and even fewer choices in life. The assistance provided by Fair Trade offers them real opportunities to improve their situation ... Farmers or producers of such commodities as coffee, tea, cocoa, bananas, etc., are in a different position. Their produce is traded on the world market in huge quantities making them vulnerable to fluctuations in price and demand and to the impact of the international trade rules made at the World Trade Organisation. By trading in these commodities, Fair Trade Organisations are able to make a difference to the lives of the farmers concerned.

Whether crafts or commodities, fair trading functions to improve the conditions of disadvantaged and marginalized people – groups that are often targets of commercial exploitation. Fair Trade works to engage the poor in productive enterprises and share value and power with them. In partnering with community-based organizations that represent the neediest members of a society, such as women, the disabled, or ethnic minorities, Fair Trade offers a humane contrast to businesses that "race to the bottom" to find the cheapest labor and services across the value chain.

Another element of this preference for disadvantaged and small-scale producers is that Fair Trade tries to correct some imbalances in the free trade system. Alex Nicholls and Charlotte Opal in *Fair Trade: Market-Driven Ethical Consumption* lay out some of the obstacles producers confront:

Lack of access to local and export markets because of lack of transportation and infrastructure
Lack of information about world prices
Lack of information about quality and industry requirements
Lack of access to financial markets for competitive credit and capital
Inability to respond easily to market forces given the incredible risks to livelihood
Weak legal systems that do not protect producer rights

Organizations committed to Fair Trade recognize and try to remove or work around these barriers. Conventional companies, unless particularly socially responsible, often do not concern themselves with the challenges faced by producers.

How messages are communicated to customers is also a distinction between Fair Trade and conventional trade. As analyst Naomi Klein critically reveals in *No Logo*, multinational corporations invest profits in sophisticated branding efforts to sell not just products but also identities. Product placements in Hollywood movies, celebrity endorsements, and symbolic associations between, for example, the Nike swoosh and the ability to "Just Do It" create demand for products whose value is manifest not necessarily in their inherent function but in their reputation. Although fair traders also use advertising and marketing techniques, central to these efforts is improving the lives of producer partners and creating connections with consumers. Successful Fair Trade businesses not only inform consumers about the impact of their purchases, but they also offer proof that conventional business plans are not the only way to achieve success. Identity formation is related to helping consumers associate themselves with trading principles and practices that address problems of poverty and inequity. When consumers become champions of the causes addressed by Fair Trade they are also more motivated to resist the appeal of cheap, mass-produced products, or at least to consider those purchases in a Fair Trade context.

While the contrasts between Fair Trade and conventional trade are striking, it is important to keep in mind that the Fair Trade model is not a remedy for all the ills of free market business practices. Fair Trade can be a powerful force in the hand-harvested and handcrafted sectors of an economy, but in a pure sense it is not necessarily applicable to manufacturing, except in isolated cases such as Fair Trade sports balls. However, as consumers, we can use the principles of Fair Trade to make decisions about which purchases to make. There are tools such as the Global Reporting Initiative and the Dow & Jones Sustainability Indexes to help evaluate corporate business practices. When buying a vehicle, we can consider fuel efficiency and its relationship to pollution, as well as style, price, and convenience. When shopping for clothes, we can seek out manufacturers who have made a commitment to avoid sweatshops by allowing unions to organize in the workplace. As shareholders, we can use resolutions and other decision-making tools to monitor corporate codes of conduct. We can bypass multinational corporations that control much of the world's food production by participating in community-supported agriculture structures that commit to regular purchases from local family farms.

Table 2. Comparison between fair and conventional trade

Fair Trade	Conventional trade
Concerns for people, the planet, and profit predominate	Profit is the overriding concern
Advance credit allows for income during times of cultivation or production	Payment is received at time of shipment or typically within 30, 60, or 90 days
Technical assistance and training, along with social premiums, investment in low-income communities and opportunities for self-determination	Corporate investment in a community is limited to building skill sets for use in commercial enterprises or takes the form of corporate philanthropy
Disadvantaged groups such as women and ethnic minorities are made partners in the Fair Trade supply network	Supply chain seeks out lowest cost labor and raw material items, often through exploitative middlemen
Consumer education and advocacy leads to socially responsible business innovations	Marketing is directed at increasing profitability

Dave Tilford of the Center for a New American Dream puts it this way:

> Whether it's underpaying workers and producers, or extracting resources in a way that destroys ecosystems and devastates local communities, we make it too easy for unethical corporations to leave environmental and social damage off the balance sheets, to extract resources and dispose of waste unsustainably while letting society foot the bill. We should all become more informed and participate in [both economic and] political process in a way that supports better practices.

The decision to exercise judgment and use the influence of consumer dollars is a true freedom of capitalism and its conventional trading practices. In fact, as Fair Trade shop co-owner Marco Hernandez says, "You deserve to have an alternative. You have the right to choices." In the end, the *freedom* of "free trade" is truly exercised through values-based choices. Consumers make choices each and every day about how to spend money and how to exercise power along various value chains: those that clothe us, inform us, transport and nourish us. Fair Trade, with its intentional and persistent focus on empowerment and the transfer of value, is a means by which consumers can recognize the type of pond – or economy – they are swimming in and how they can make conscious decisions about spending money.

3

Why is Fair Trade so popular?

Overview: Fair Trade has grown exponentially in recent years. Many market-related reasons, such as the multiplication of product lines, can be credited with this success. But looking beyond statistics and advertising efforts, we see that Fair Trade is also energized by the stories behind the products.

When I consider why Fair Trade is increasing in popularity, why it draws so many different kinds of people to the movement, the core factor for me is the people and institutions involved. Let's move from the abstract principles of chapter two to a view of how Fair Trade is embodied in everyday life and how these stories take their place in the context of related social movements.

Where are those people from anyway? Crafts in Chile

Like many fair traders, Winnie Lira Letelier is an unassuming but feisty advocate for the craftswomen she represents. Her tone is quiet and her attitude is self-effacing; however, her resolve to promote fairly traded crafts – even in competition with multinational giants such as the Disney Corporation – never falters.

Letelier is the executive director of Fundación Solidaridad (see box) in Santiago, Chile, whose mission is to raise the quality of life of artisans through Fair Trade and micro-enterprise. Founded in 1974, Fundación Solidaridad works with approximately 500 poor Chileans, almost ninety percent of whom are women. I met Letelier at a Fair Trade Symposium held parallel to the World Trade Organization meetings in Cancun, Mexico, in 2003. At the symposium, she shared the following story about how the women of Fundación Solidaridad went toe-to-toe with toy makers to win a government contract:

As in all countries of the world, the Chilean state spends thousands of millions of dollars a year for the purchase of many products …According to the law, the bids are open to all. By order of the World Trade Organization, and following the most sacred laws of the free market, everyone, Chilean or foreigner, can participate … [T]o compete in these public bid conditions is to face … the "unavoidable multinational," which can underbid anyone with products made in China or Taiwan.

Fundación Solidaridad was inspired to compete with the giants one day when a school director visited a shop and mentioned that it would be a very good idea for children in primary schools to play with dolls dressed as Chileans, and not with a "mindless, sexless Barbie doll." Fundación Solidaridad decided to compete for contracts from the Ministry of Education by offering culturally appropriate and anatomically correct dolls for use in health classes. Letelier recounted for me the results of one contract bidding process:

> At the opening of the state public bids, the representatives of the producers sit waiting in the room where an official of the Ministry will open the envelopes with the bids. There, next to us, we see the representatives of Mattel, Fisher-Price, Disney Company, and others. If it were not so hard sometimes, due to the irritating difference between them and us, this often becomes even funny. When the notary in charge announces that Fundación Solidaridad is the winner for some item and the women hug each other, showing their happiness, the representatives of the large companies look around nervously. They do not understand what is going on. So, they ask, "Where are those people from, anyway?" In spite of this disparaging remark, we continue fighting to demonstrate that when poor artisans are organized, they can be state suppliers. This is done with products of high quality, friendly to the culture of our people, and manufactured according to the norms of the Fair Trade Ethical Code.

In twenty percent of its attempts, Fundación Solidaridad wins contracts based on quality and price. In some years, these contracts provide as much as forty percent of the organization's revenue. Fundación Solidaridad's ability not only to secure government contracts, but more importantly to help poor artisans work themselves out of poverty, is a

Figure 2 Patricia Hildago of Fundación Solidaridad proudly displays a culturally appropriate doll.

key feature of Fair Trade that attracts consumers. In the United States and Europe, consumers find Fundación Solidaridad products through the work of Intermón Oxfam, SERRV International, Solidar Monde, and Traidcraft Exchange, and in retail stores, such as Ten Thousand Villages, or in the A Greater Gift (formerly SERRV) catalog. Each product uses a hangtag to give information about the product and the craftswoman who created it. This short story informs and inspires the consumers and connects them to the life of the artisan.

Time and time again the stories behind the products serve to build and sustain Fair Trade's popularity. Knowing that a purchase can help a group of impoverished women compete successfully with multinationals fuels the dedication of fair traders. These success stories also add threads to the web of relationships that make Fair Trade a vibrant social phenomenon. Along with hundreds of other advocates, I was inspired by the women of Fundación Solidaridad at an international conference. We carried the story back to our respective countries. We offered the case as a model for promoting small, democratic businesses over mammoth, impersonal corporations.

Good cocoa growers and business owners: a Ghanaian cooperative

The technical assistance and market access enjoyed by members of Fundación Solidaridad are familiar features of the Fair Trade system. However, a new model of producer empowerment capturing attention is worker-owned Fair Trade businesses. The Day Chocolate Company, which is owned in part by the Kuapa Kokoo cocoa association in Ghana, is a prime example. Consumers like knowing they are helping producers move out of poverty while also assisting in their greater participation in the financial enterprises involved in making and selling their products.

"In an unprecedented international joint venture" in 1998, the Day Chocolate Company was established by Kuapa Kokoo (see box), the Body Shop, the British non-governmental organization, Twin Trading (see chapter seven), and other supportive partners – including the British Department for International Development – to launch a distinctive Fair Trade chocolate brand called Divine. By owning a share of the Day Chocolate Company with full representation on its board of directors, Kuapa Kokoo goes beyond the typical Fair Trade framework of a more equitable supply chain by securing a significant measure of control of that chain through farmer governance and decision-making. This model helps the Fair Trade consumer move beyond a charity mode of "buying without guilt" to enabling buyers to support companies that are partially owned by producers. In recognition of this model Day Chocolate has received the British Government Millennium Award.

Divine Chocolate has become a darling of the Fair Trade movement in the United States, particularly among people of faith. In 2006, Lutheran World Relief (L.W.R.) invested $270,000 to become a founding partner of Divine Chocolate U.S.A., a successor organization that follows the

FUNDACIÓN SOLIDARIDAD

With roots in the Cooperation Committee for Peace in Chile, Fundación Solidaridad was founded to increase the earnings, market insertion, and social participation of people, families, and groups who, by their own efforts, seek to overcome poverty and improve their quality of life by producing handicrafts in workshops and micro-businesses. The beneficiaries are:

community women's organizations
community youth groups
indigenous groups of Mapuches, Aymaras
young artisans with learning difficulties
family businesses

The foundation offers advice and training in:

design
production processes
calculation of costs and prices
quality control
organizational development
creation of product sector networks

The goods are marketed internationally and are also available for sale in two retail shops in Chile.

Source: www.fundacionsolidaridad.cl

Day Chocolate model. L.W.R. took this remarkable step, according to Brenda Meier, director for Parish and Community Engagement, to embrace a different approach to development that supports farmers not only as producers but also as owners. L.W.R.'s ally, Catholic Relief Services, has adopted the Divine brand as their preferred brand of Fair Trade chocolate marketed to some sixty-seven million U.S. Catholics.

Figure 3 Kuapa Kokoo member Helena Bempong holding a candy bar created by her chocolate company.

Divine is also a secular phenomenon. In less than a decade, Divine has taken hold of consumer imagination in the United Kingdom through its commercial partnerships with the Co-op supermarket chain and Starbucks U.K. and the celebrity support of Comic Relief. In the United States Kwabena Ohemeng-Tinyase, managing director of Kuapa Kokoo, was the keynote speaker at the first Fair Trade Futures conference held in the United States in September 2005. The conference attracted 750 consumers and businesses from twenty different countries. Ohemeng-Tinyase described the political, social, and economic benefits of Fair Trade as "enormous," particularly as they relate to equal opportunities for women. Ohemeng-Tinyase also underscored the value brought by the increase in business skills throughout the association.

The country of Ghana is ranked 119 out of 162 in terms of development level. Consumer belief that systematic poverty is addressed through associations, such as Kuapa Kokoo, at the individual and community level is another motivating force behind the success of Fair Trade.

Off the shelf and into the basket: consumer crusade in Canada

Artisans and farmers can produce high-quality products that reach Northern markets through Fair Trade and mainstream channels, but if no one buys the items, the Fair Trade model falters. Consumers who are committed to purchasing the products and spreading word of their availability are critical in the growth of the Fair Trade movement in North America.

In 2000, Bruce Morton of Barrie, Ontario, Canada, noticed Fair Trade certified coffee arriving in natural and specialty stores. Curious about the Fair Trade concept, he began Internet research and discovered the Fair Trade Resource Network and other organizations. The discovery convinced Morton that Fair Trade was a better system because profits and the Fair Trade social premium arrived in communities directly and benefited children and families. After meeting with staff of TransFair Canada, the certifier of Fair Trade products in Canada, Morton decided that in order for Fair Trade to succeed more conscious consumers like himself needed to know of its existence. "The coffee was on the shelf," according to Morton, "but it wasn't coming off the shelf into the basket."

Starting out with a framed photo of the TransFair Canada label and some informational fliers, Bruce approached a health food store with this proposition, "Look, if I buy a bag of coffee, will you brew it this weekend and give samples away with some educational material?" Because retailers are always looking for low-cost ways to sell more product, his neighborhood store agreed. Then after a couple of successful weekends, Morton said to the store, "Hey, how about I stand next to the samples and answer any customer questions?" As the retailers were not very well educated about Fair Trade – primarily stocking it because of organic blends – the addition of Bruce Morton as a Fair Trade spokesperson was welcomed.

KUAPA KOKOO

In 1993, the late Nana Frimpong Abebrese, a farmers' representative on the Ghanaian Cocoa Marketing Board, was worried about how the recent free trade entries of private companies into the cocoa trading system would affect poor farmers. With assistance from Twin Trading in London and S.N.V., a Dutch non-governmental organization, Abebrese and other farmers established the Kuapa Kokoo association. In the Twi language, *Kuapa Kokoo* means "good cocoa grower" and reflects a desire to avoid the corruption that had been rampant in the cocoa market.

With some 45,000 members in 1,200 Ghanaian villages, Kuapa Kokoo aims for:

increased power and representation within the market for the farmers
social, economic, and political empowerment
enhanced women's participation in all its affairs
environmentally sustainable production processes

Although not all of its cocoa is sold on the Fair Trade market, the Fair Trade price ($1600 per ton) plus social premium ($150 per ton) has contributed to creating better living conditions for members of Kuapa Kokoo. Investments, such as school construction, provision of clean water and sewage facilities, and support of income generation projects, have been made to benefit families and communities.

Source: www.kuapakokoogh.com

By this time, Morton had connected with Oxfam Canada, secured a folding table and a drip maker, and found himself devoting at least one Saturday morning a month to spreading the Fair Trade message. "Without exception," he explained, "sales increased and the retailers were asking me back for next week." Morton believes that, in addition to the great-tasting coffee, the public responded because they appreciate help

Figure 4 In-store demos by volunteers such as Bruce Morton build awareness and knowledge of Fair Trade.

sorting through advertising claims and charitable appeals. "The concept that we are investing in cooperatives to help people to develop their skills, build their businesses, send their kids to universities makes a lot of sense [to the public]." Fair Trade awareness in Canada received a major boost in 2004 when Kicking Horse Coffee Roasters of British Columbia teamed up with Neal Brothers Distributors to introduce their Fair Trade coffee to mainstream grocery stores in Ontario. Neal Brothers was approached by Morton and was eager to support Fair Trade demos. In-store demos could now reach as many as 100 consumers on a Saturday morning versus forty or so in the smaller health food stores.

Although Bruce Morton can't personally meet the demand for Saturday-morning education sessions, he has been able to spread his technique with the help of Fair Trade Toronto, which does coffee demos during World Fair Trade Week in May and other special events. The ability to make a positive impact as a consumer, in partnership with Fair Trade Organizations, is another dimension of Fair Trade's popularity. As we considered in chapter one, one billion people in the world live on less than a dollar a day. This figure represents not only a daily struggle to fight off starvation and disease, but it also points to glaring inequalities in which residents of high-income countries live in relative luxury. With Fair Trade, consumers can help bridge the wealth gap and reach farmers and artisans who desperately need Fair Trade to survive and thrive.

Beyond the individual story: one of many movements

These profiles are discrete examples of Fair Trade in action. Without these kinds of individual commitments and successes – taken in concert with like-minded allies and partners – Fair Trade's recent growth would be not much more than a commercial success story, and perhaps a fleeting one at that. Although the popularity of Fair Trade is measured by exponential sales rates, success and sustainability are demonstrated by more than sales figures alone.

Consumers who join individuals and institutions such as Winnie Lira Letelier, Bruce Morton and Kuapa Kokoo as Fair Traders are aligning themselves with and adding to the vision of complementary political and social movements, most notably the environmental – or green – movement, the labor movement, and the trade justice movement. It is no surprise that there is an affinity amongst various movements. The priorities of Fair Trade mirror other efforts to redress injustice and exploitation. Indeed, one of the beauties of Fair Trade is the comprehensiveness of its concerns. Within the F.I.N.E. definition of Fair Trade (see chapter 1), we see threads of environmentalism, labor concerns, and trade justice. And those threads are woven by unique individuals who have emerged as the proponents of, and participants in, Fair Trade.

A research study of Fair – then called alternative – Trade Organizations published in 1999 by Mary Ann Littrell and Marsha Ann Dickson helped define the Fair Trade customer, and a consideration of those characteristics reveals an intersection of values. Littrell and Dickson associated Fair Trade consumers with the term "cultural creatives." Cultural creatives are described as college-educated, middle-aged, and middle-class. They are mostly female and are often volunteers in their communities who engage in global concerns through travel and use of various news media. "Values of community building, ecological sustainability, abhorrence of violence, and attraction to the foreign and exotic guide their lives." They are similar to a market niche more recently identified as L.O.H.A.S. or those who embrace Lifestyles of Health and Sustainability. The National Marketing Institute reports that twenty-seven percent of all American adults can be classified as L.O.H.A.S. Similarly, in their textbook *Fair Trade: Market-Driven Ethical Consumption*, Nichols and Opal report that sixty-five percent of U.K. consumers consider themselves "green or ethical." We will start our consideration of movement overlap with the environmental movement.

Environmentalism and Fair Trade

In the United States, some credit the birth of the environmental movement to the publication of Rachel Carson's 1960 critique *Silent Spring*, while others point to environmentalism as an outgrowth of the civil rights and anti-war movements of the 1960s and early 1970s. The founding of organizations, such as Greenpeace in the early 1970s, and the push for conservation prompted by the energy crisis of 1977 are also forces in the development of a movement focused on protecting the planet. As we shall see later, some of the Fair Trade food labeling requirements relate to environmental practices. By 2005, organizations, such as the Sierra Club, had incorporated the rhetoric of Fair Trade into their agendas, and the Organic Consumers Association intentionally aligned itself with Fair Trade through a campaign that included promotion of Fair Trade coffee at Starbucks cafes.

As these movements work more and more in tandem, Fair Trade food products are increasingly becoming organic. The most popular Fair Trade product in the United States, certified coffee, is also organic in sixty percent of cases. This reflects consumer demands as the global market for organics in the United States grew to as much as $31 billion in 2003. There are a number of reasons why the organic movement has grown, health concerns of consumers primary among them. As Bruce

Morton's supermarket campaign demonstrated, when consumers know they can shop with their values and priorities, they do. Fair Trade businesses and producers also embrace the benefits gained from eliminating synthetic pesticides and fertilizers on both environmental and social grounds.

Cooperative Coffees, a whole bean coffee importer committed to purchasing only Fair Trade coffee, also only purchases organic and transitional organic beans. Tripp Pomeroy, outreach chair of Cooperative Coffees, explains, "Sustainable cultivation techniques and Fair Trade's long-term viability are inextricably connected. Socio-economic development and stability literally depend on sustaining a healthy, productive environment. Without organic systems and standards, farmers wear out the very resource on which they depend for their livelihood: their land." Pomeroy points out that the members of Cooperative Coffees have learned from their producer partners that organic systems are viewed by most producers as a return to the traditional method of coffee farming. Organic cultivation represents a return to a "better way" to farm and teaches a lesson to the developed countries of the world: pay attention to and respect knowledge that resides with small producers – they may know something we do not. Perhaps most importantly, traditional organic practices protect farmers and communities from the harmful effects of conventional fertilizers and pesticides.

Organic farming also produces a higher quality product that appeals to discerning consumers. These values and market reactions are not limited to coffee. In the United Kingdom, the retail value for environmentally sustainable Fair Trade fruit grew 206% from 2000 to 2003.

In the craft sectors, the pursuit of environmental sustainability is in some cases more complicated than standardized organic or integrated pest management practices but no less important. Fair Trade Organizations (F.T.O.) and their producer partners strive to eliminate toxins, such as leads in paint or poisons in dyes, in order to protect the producer, the consumer, and the environment. The development assistance and training provided by F.T.O.s allow producers to create products that meet consumer demands for sustainability while protecting health and safety.

In 2003, SERRV International, an F.T.O. based in Madison, Wisconsin (see chapter four), adopted a policy to source fast-growing, sustainable wood products from Kenya. Machakos District Cooperative Union

(M.D.C.U.), one of SERRV's Kenyan partners, had established a tree nursery to address the issue of scarcity of wood in Kenya. When M.D.C.U. needed to expand the nursery to meet the rising demand, SERRV funded the purchase of 1,000 seedlings as a sustainable solution to nursery expansions that would provide raw materials for future wood carvings.

Although the premise of the Fair Trade movement is based on the reality that individuals need to consume goods, an environmental sensibility pervades its adherents. Consumers who have embraced the mantra of "reduce, reuse, recycle" often seek to give their business to producers and businesses committed to environmentally friendly practices through Fair Trade principles. At the same time, Fair Traders struggle with the environmental costs such as those involved in sourcing Fair Trade items from often distant countries requiring the significant use of fossil-fuels for transport. Alliance with green advocates helps the movement seek expertise and innovation in confronting such realities in an earth-friendly way.

Sweat-free movement

Labor activists in the anti-sweatshop or sweat-free movement focus their attention on the people who convert the planet's resources into manufactured goods. A description of the work of the International Labor Rights Fund (I.L.R.F.) summarizes the concerns of the sweat-free activists:

> In the new global economy, corporations from developed countries are increasingly moving their production to developing countries, where they can take advantage of cheap labor under sweatshop conditions. Workers must toil extremely long hours in labor intensive jobs with low pay and often unsanitary and unsafe conditions. In many countries, there is little or no labor law enforcement, and many workers are prevented from joining organizations to advance their interests. Even more alarming, an estimated 250 million children between the ages of five and fourteen are working around the world.

I.L.R.F. and other non-governmental organizations campaign against such abuse and encourage consumers to boycott companies that are particularly egregious in their reliance on sweatshop conditions to increase profitability.

Many consumers associate this type of "sweatshop activism" in the United States with the revelation in 1995 that U.S. television celebrity Kathy Lee Gifford – who had developed a public persona as a dedicated and doting mother – endorsed a clothing line that was produced by children as young as thirteen working fifteen-hour days. When the allegations were revealed, consumer repulsion from the Kathy Lee brand led to significant changes in the product's supply chain. Although the sweat-free movement can actually be traced back to widespread textile strikes early in the twentieth century, the general public had not been agitated until the Kathy Lee scandal.

University students quickly seized the issue, especially as it related to the manufacture of licensed university apparel. A student who had interned at U.N.I.T.E. (Union of Needletrades, Industrial and Textile Employees), Tico Almeida, began a campaign at Duke University pressing for a code of conduct for all manufacturers of clothing and accessories that bore the Duke logo. A short three years later, the United Students Against Sweatshops had formed and soon created a companion organization called the Workers Rights Consortium (W.R.C.). Mainstream corporations, such as Nike, had adopted codes of conduct in response to pressure tactics and boycotts. However, the students and others engaged in anti-sweatshop activities felt those measures to be inadequate. W.R.C. devised a stronger response to worrisome labor conditions by monitoring facilities in response to specific worker complaints. This acknowledgment of workers as the source of information and power – similar to the structure of the Day Chocolate Company – indicates respect in both sweat-free and Fair Trade arenas for the voice of workers.

At the community level, sweat-free communities (S.F.C.) began to arise. Initiated in Bangor, Maine, S.F.C.s are efforts by citizens to ensure that their tax dollars are not used to procure clothing manufactured in sweatshops for use by public servants, such as police officers and firefighters. This is similar to European efforts such as the Clean Clothes Campaign. Approximately thirty-five local U.S. municipalities have adopted policies designed to filter out the worst abusers of factory workers' rights. In 2005, San Francisco, California, passed a sweat-free ordinance requiring that clothing purchased by the city's contractors and vendors abide by a "sweat-free" code of conduct, which includes a living wage requirement and a ban on child labor.

Sweatshop-free items are sometimes called Fair Trade because of the wage and working condition concerns. However, use of the term is not entirely accurate, and there has actually been some disconnection at best, and friction at worst, between the sweat-free and Fair Trade movements. On the one hand, unions were initially concerned that Fair Trade advocates were promoting or aiding the shift of manufacturing to overseas or offshore locations because the Fair Trade movement is primarily concerned with international trade. More recently there have been concerns about the ability of workers to organize in the context of Fair Trade. The Fair Trade model relies, for the most part, on small-scale farmers working through a cooperative model. Pro-labor advocates debate what such a model has to offer landless farmworkers seeking unionized employment on a banana plantation, for example. With the exception of sports balls or composite products such as chocolate, the Fair Trade model is not strictly applicable to the manufacturing sector because it is focused on small-scale production, often based in homes or in rural workshops, not in factories. The supply chain for a product, such as a T-shirt, is far more complicated than that for a farm product, such as coffee, so Fair Trade criteria may not be sufficient.

These points of divergence do not necessarily mean there is a conflict between fair traders and labor organizers but it does sometimes blur points of convergence. Together, fair traders and sweat-free activists work against oversimplifying both the complex Fair Trade model and the myriad of situations that are faced by workers around the world fighting for economic justice. Because Fair Trade principles are so comprehensive in their concerns, the Fair Trade model is sympathetic to, and aligned with, the labor movement, and efforts are being made to bring the two movements together, especially at the local level through work with S.F.C.s.

At the worker level, the Sweat-free and Fair Trade movements have found positive intersections. For example, the Nueva Vida women's sewing cooperative in Nicaragua produces a line of sweatshop-free clothing for customers, such as Maggie's Organics, a well-known clothing company based in the United States. The Nueva Vida women, as owners and leaders of the cooperative, guarantee fair wages and good working conditions at the factory that they constructed, by hand, with help from an international development organization, the Center for Development in Central America. The cooperative declared its operations a Fair Trade Zone after the Nicaraguan government awarded it the benefits of a traditional free trade zone, namely duty-free imports and tax breaks. By claiming both free trade perks and adhering to Fair Trade principles, Nueva Vida offers a workable alternative to conventional trading regimes.

Trade justice

Advocate concerns over the pursuit of conventional, or free-trade agreements, have created another movement that has kinship with Fair Trade: the Trade Justice Movement (T.J.M.). Begun in the wake of the successful Jubilee 2000, a campaign to reduce the debt burdens of developing countries, the T.J.M. represents a range of British non-governmental organizations advocating for trade policies that work to keep the concerns of the poor above those of the multinational corporations. Similar coalitions have been organized in the Americas. As we heard in Letelier's story, trade agreements shape the business environment for small-scale producers and are thus a critical concern for those who want to make trade fairer at the micro and macro levels.

In its founding document, *For Whose Benefit? Making Trade Work for People and the Planet*, the T.J.M. enumerates the principles it stands for, including international trade and democracy. Its main critique of the current free trade system is that it has:

> Favoured the narrow commercial interests of the most powerful trading nations and the largest corporations, at the expense of the wider public interest and smaller economic enterprises. In order to rebalance the global trading system, international trade rules and institutions must take their place within the broad system of international agreements aimed at sustainable development, poverty eradication and the promotion of human rights, and recognise the importance of local and regional trade as an engine for sustainable development and poverty eradication.

This focus on economic development through the efforts of small-scale producers, concerns for the environment, and commitment to human rights makes the T.J.M. a natural complement to the Fair Trade movement. Indeed, *For Whose Benefit?* specifically calls for "fairness" in the trade regime with a "pro-poor" orientation. Many of the advocacy organizations that have taken a prominent role in promoting Fair Trade, particularly in the United Kingdom, such as ActionAid and Save the Children, as well as Fair Trade organizations themselves, such as Cafédirect and Traidcraft, are members of the T.J.M. These organizations have a collective membership of nine million, roughly matching the population of Sweden. Aligning themselves with a variety of political campaigns, those advocating for trade justice are broadly concerned with the everyday realities faced by millions of artisans and farmers who are trying to use the Fair Trade model to confront their own poverty, protect their land and biosphere, and create an alternative method of conducting trade.

On November 2, 2005, as a round of World Trade Organization negotiations in Hong Kong approached, more than 8,000 campaigners associated with various organizations affiliated with T.J.M., as well as the Global Campaign Against Poverty, lobbied 375 members of Parliament in the United Kingdom. The event, which demanded that the UK Government and European Union (EU) partners pull back from insistence that developing countries open their markets, was the largest lobbying effort in the history of modern British democracy.

Free to be fair

A conservationist supporting sustainable agriculture, a student protesting sweatshops, and a policy analyst debunking institutions, such as the World Bank, could all claim membership in the Fair Trade movement. Underscored by the inspiring stories that began this chapter, synergetic relations to other justice movements are part of why Fair Trade is thriving. As Fair Trade researcher Laura T. Raynolds has noted, "The overall goal of [fair] trade is to counter the organization of production and trade around abstract market principles that devalue and exploit disadvantaged peoples and the environment."

Yann Martel, author of the Booker Prize-winning book *Life of Pi*, was Canada's spokesperson for World Fair Trade Week in May 2004. In an editorial, Martel likened Fair Trade to the I-Thou Relationship defined by philosopher Martin Buber. Buber had taught that relationships are not "a posture or attitude, but a mode of existence" characterized by engagement, equality, and trust. They are contrary to the prevalent I-It relationships in society that diminish humanity, commodify the environment, and promote value-less materialism. Martel notes, "We live in a world that is at present dominated by It-ness, where profit and convenience often seem to matter more than quality of life ... The I-Thou [relationship] of Fair Trade is a way of reclaiming our humanity and that of those who are less fortunate."

Fair Trade is successful and will continue to be an attractive social force because of the likes of Winnie Lira Letelier, Bruce Morton, and the farmers of Kuapa Kokoo. Reinforced by its alliances to like-minded movements, Fair Trade offers a framework in which to exercise freedom as a consumer and as a human being.

4

Fair Trade principles and practices

Overview: although there is growing awareness of Fair Trade products, understanding the definition of Fair Trade – if there is one single definition – can be difficult. This chapter looks at the core principles of Fair Trade, how those principles are interpreted, and what role labels play in the movement.

Soon after a volunteer stint with the Mut Vitz coffee cooperative in Chiapas, Mexico, I was sharing my understandings about the Fair Trade model with an old friend. After hearing my description of the ability of Fair Trade to transform the lives, not only of disadvantaged people around the world, but also of wealthy consumers who had been lulled into unconscious consumerism, the friend responded, "This sounds wonderful! I have to replace my refrigerator. Where can I get a Fair Trade one?" This interaction was an early lesson in the need to explain persuasively and *completely* the Fair Trade model without falling into the trap of suggesting that Fair Trade is the solution to all of society's ills.

As we saw in chapter one, F.I.N.E., a consortium of Fair Trade associations, uses a description of Fair Trade as a partnership and alternative model of doing business that specifically helps disadvantaged people. The F.I.N.E. definition reflects a broad-based understanding of what Fair Trade means to many non-profit organizations and Fair Trade businesses. However, when designing and assessing Fair Trade partnerships, specific criteria are needed. The Fair Trade Federation (F.T.F.), an association of Fair Trade businesses in North America, uses a set of Fair Trade criteria that constitutes the interrelated principles that define the values of the Fair Trade movement.

In the purest sense, these or similar criteria are embraced by all the actors involved in Fair Trade: the producers, the buyers, the transporters, the retailers, and ultimately, the consumers. I use the F.T.F. criteria as a point of reference for our consideration of what Fair Trade is. However, many organizations frame and explain the criteria differently according to their specific audience, customers, or stakeholders.

Principles of Fair Trade

Let's consider the core principles that make the value transfer and network development possible, as expressed by F.T.F.

Fair wages

The first criterion of Fair Trade is that the producer of a craft item or food product is paid a fair wage in the local economy where she or he is working. The most clear cut example is the case of coffee, where Fairtrade Labeling Organizations International (F.L.O.) has determined that to cover the cost of production and invest in the community a farmer cooperative should receive at least $1.35 a pound, reflecting a ten cent premium added to the floor price of $1.25. If the coffee has been grown organically, the Fair Trade price increases to $1.55 in recognition of the additional costs associated with environmentally friendly

---

FAIR TRADE CRITERIA ARE:

Paying a fair wage in the local context
Offering employees opportunities for advancement
Providing equal employment opportunities for all people, particularly the most disadvantaged
Engaging in environmentally sustainable practices
Being open to public accountability
Building long-term trade relationships
Providing healthy and safe working conditions within the local context
Providing financial and technical assistance to producers whenever possible

Source: Fair Trade Federation

agricultural practices. The ten cent social premium does not go to increasing the income of the farmers directly but instead is used to invest in community development. For example, in Tanzania, the Kilimanjaro Native Co-operative Union Ltd. used the social premium to establish a cooperative bank to finance economic projects and an education fund that benefits both children and adult members.

The importance of the commitment to the Fair Trade price was dramatically proven during the coffee crisis that began in 2000. Oxfam International described the crisis this way:

> When the international coffee price crashed to thirty year lows in 2001, millions of coffee farmers around the world faced hardships and reduced incomes. In countries like Ethiopia where significant portions of foreign revenue come from coffee exports, the crisis left farming families unable to pay for education and health care. Throughout Central America, an estimated 600,000 jobs on coffee farms were lost. These conditions have been linked to migration and increased production of illicit crops, giving rise to a vicious cycle of social instability at the local and regional levels.

I was in Mexico in late 1999 when the coffee prices began their descent. Although I was privileged to be among Fair Trade coffee farmers, poverty in the coffee-growing region was rampant. I saw families with six or seven members packed into homes with one or two rooms, struggling with poor nutrition, in need of consistent health care, and eager for the income that could translate their hard work into living wages. These farmers of the MutVitz cooperative, like so many other producers, toil against incredible odds and sometimes seemingly inscrutable forces to live and prosper. It was in observing the capacities and possibilities in these farming communities that I became convinced of the potential for economic development through the growth of the Fair Trade market.

And, in fact, the Fair Trade coffee market has grown in the years since my time in Mexico. TransFair USA reports that since 1999 Fair Trade Certified™ coffee sales grew by twenty-five percent in 2009. In recent years, the coffee crisis has diminished to the extent that prices have risen, reflecting the cyclical nature of commodity trading. When the coffee market recovers and the conventional market price of coffee rises above the floor price of $1.25, fair traders continue to pay the additional five cent social premium as an indication of their long-term partnership and as an ongoing investment in the coffee-producing communities. The producers, for their part, are also expected to honor their contracted obligations to their Fair Trade cooperatives.

It is important to note that the minimum Fair Trade price is not a system that can be used for craft production. The steps in production of stationery, for example, may differ greatly if the paper is made in Africa or in Asia. The raw materials may be different in terms of type of wood or recycled matter. The process for preparing the paper varies according to who makes it and where. And, the design embellishments will reflect unique cultural traditions when color and other style choices are made. Therefore, it is exceedingly difficult to stipulate that a handmade birthday card should always cost, say, $1.00.

These difficulties were clear to me when visiting paper making enterprises in Madagascar. An orphanage for abandoned children and

Figure 5 A young woman making stationery in Madagascar.

"delinquent" girls had set up a workshop for producing recycled greeting cards. The cards were made directly from office paper shredded by embassies in the capital city, Antananarivo, where the orphanage was located. The high school age girls incorporated local fibers in their designs. They were quite different from a set of greeting cards that I purchased from another workshop in Madagascar that did not have access to surplus paper, but was able to purchase stock card for cutting. The stock was then overlaid with embroidered cloth depicting agricultural scenes from the countryside. Although both products were technically greeting cards from the same country, the source of materials, the method of production, and the labor required to produce them varied greatly.

This lack of uniformity, however, gives the buyers and sellers of crafts an opportunity for further dialogue and to negotiate transparently. When working together to determine the value of a product, the artisan – most usually a woman – is able to identify and assess the value of her work and creativity. With her buyer partner, she is able to base prices on market realities that she may not otherwise be aware of. One of the critiques of the conventional trading system is that producers often lack access to information about what the market will bear and thus, are at the mercy of middlemen looking only to increase their own profit margins. Yet, in the Fair Trade system, I have heard potential buyers tell producers, "You can get more for that handbag. In the United States similar products sell for twice as much." Although it might be tempting to look for a label that indicates, "All Fair Trade handbags cost X," the lack of uniformity is a testament to the potential of partnership and give-and-take relationships among fair traders. This dialogue is also important for consumers like you to keep in mind when weighing purchasing decisions. With Fair Trade, you have more certainty that the producer had a voice in determining the value of the product given the realities of her life. Later in the book, we will look at other ways, such as using the Fair Trade Wage Guide, in which producers can assume more control of the pricing process.

Good working conditions

Whatever the price negotiated between the buyer and the producer, another element figured into the equation is the condition of the workplace.

Fair Trade farmers and artisans are small-scale producers. They may have home-based businesses, modest community workshops, or small plots of family-owned land. This small-scale production benefits the legions of poor people, who live in rural settings without access to or skills for manufacturing jobs. Fair traders pledge to make the working environment – be it a home-based business or a communal workspace – safe and healthy according to local standards, and to make sure that there is no exploitative child labor as defined by the International Labor Organization. This last point is important because child labor is rightly a concern of consumers and advocates. RUGMARK International, for example, works to end illegal child labor in the South Asian carpet industry by certifying manufacturers and providing educational opportunities for children removed from abusive rug workshops. The origins of RUGMARK parallel the advocacy of Iqbal Masih, who had escaped from slave labor in a rug workshop and spent his brief freedom galvanizing the anti-child labor movement in the carpet industry before being shot at the age of twelve. Other organizations, such as the International Labor Rights Fund and Global Exchange, have worked to eliminate abusive child labor from the cocoa industry. These are important attempts to keep corporations accountable for their labor practices, but they should not be painted with too broad a brush.

My first day on a coffee farm in Mexico I harvested beans alongside Juan Carlos, a boy of about twelve years of age, who not only picked beans, but also hauled them in large sacks on his back to the washing basins near his family home. However, Juan Carlos was working because we were harvesting on a weekend, not when he and his siblings should have been in school. Much like family farms in the United States, some types of child labor are permissible in Fair Trade and reflect local laws and customs. Although the type and frequency may vary, what is a constant for fair traders is that producers struggling in poverty want brighter futures for their families. Increased income and social premiums make educational possibilities more likely. David Funkhouser, consumer education specialist with TransFair USA, notes, "Santiago Rivera's daughter, Yolanda, was the first member of her rural community in northern Nicaragua to graduate from high school in 2004. She is now a university student. This became possible as a result of Santiago's participation in the Fair Trade market."

Figure 6 Juan Carlos performs weekend chores on his family's farm in Mexico.

Equal opportunities for employment and advancement

In the Fair Trade marketplace, we are often introduced to images of individuals overcoming adversity through their skills and determination. While there is certainly a wealth of personal stories of lives made better through Fair Trade opportunities, the Fair Trade system notably operates on the communal level. Producers are often organized into a cooperative, which is defined by the International Co-operative Alliance as "an autonomous association of persons united voluntarily to meet their common economic, social, and cultural needs and aspirations through a jointly-owned and democratically-controlled enterprise." Some trading companies, such as La Siembra in Canada and Equal Exchange in the United States, are themselves worker-owned cooperatives.

Researcher Jennifer Wilhoit notes that "the attempt to solve common problems by combined action is at the root of cooperatives," but she underscores other benefits, such as empowerment, shared owner-ship, and democratic control. With cooperative mechanisms operating, members have the opportunity to thrive and develop their skills and leadership potential. This is particularly important in cultures that have traditionally denied opportunities to women or members of certain so-cial groups. Cooperatives are not only the domain of Fair Trade; devel-opment organizations working around the world have encouraged cooperative structures as a poverty reduction strategy. Regrettably, in the context of foreign aid transmitted through government mecha-nisms, the establishment and governance of cooperatives can become politicized and corrupted. For example, the farmers of Kuaka Kokoo, whom we learned about earlier, intentionally organized themselves as an association, not as a cooperative, because of the poor reputation co-operatives earned in Africa. Meantime, at the other end of the spectrum, Fair Trade coffee cooperatives in Nicaragua are uniquely vibrant in part due to commitments the Sandinistas made to cooperative structures during Nicaragua's civil struggles.

Whether cooperative or association, the key is that individual pro-ducers are organized in ways that multiply their impact through pooled resources and provide opportunities not otherwise available to produc-ers. Going even further, Fair Trade organizations are committed to working with the most disadvantaged groups "to oppose discrimination and ensure equality of employment opportunities for both men and women who suffer from the exploitation of their labour and the effects of poverty and racial, cultural or gender bias."

Environmental sustainability

Abel Fernandez from the Dominican Republic once told me that Fair Trade allows his cooperative to farm in ways that respect the earth. This cooperative, CONACADO, was able to use the social premiums from Fair Trade sales to pay for the costs associated with organic certification of its cocoa. He expressed his pleasure to me in this progression, not just because it opened the cooperative's product up to a wider market, but also because it allowed him to use the raw materials in his commu-nity in ways that honored his ancestors and benefited future generations.

Nevertheless, some traditional techniques – such as the use of toxic dyes or slash and burn agriculture – can be dangerous to the producers and the planet. Fair Trade buyers and producers develop environmentally friendly techniques that maintain authenticity but also promote sustainability. For example, African Home in South Africa gets its wood for traditional carvings from fallen trees, driftwood, or trees that have been introduced to the environment inappropriately and are now consuming high levels of water.

Most fair traders agree that promoting environmental sustainability is a Fair Trade principle that must be more rigorously pursued for the health of the planet and future generations. I caution, though, against using the terms environmental sustainability and organic interchangeably. Consumers have been an important force in growing the market for organic products, especially within the Fair Trade coffee sector. However, organic certification does come with certain risks. Erin Gorman, former director of Co-op America's Fair Trade Alliance, points out that organic certification can be costly to farmers. Transition to certified organic can reduce yields of products and, therefore, threaten short-term livelihoods, introducing financial instability to a family or a community. Gorman notes, "There needs to be a dialogue between Fair Traders, producer communities, and advocates about not being too dogmatic [about organics]." As of this writing, for example, coffee-buying partners of the Catholic Relief Services Fair Trade program are working with Nicaraguan producers to sell "transitional" organic coffee while the farmers work toward full certification. Consumers have a right to expect products that reflect their values, and they can rely on Fair Trade organizations and their producer partners to create products that make the most sense for the people and resources involved.

Accountability and transparency

In an era of corporate social responsibility, values, such as accountability and transparency, may seem like nothing more than buzzwords. But in practice these values are cornerstones of Fair Trade business operations. While so many businesses are scurrying to clean up tarnished images, much of the Fair Trade movement shines with its commitment to fair business practices. These practices not only address economic and social justice issues, but they also improve business ethics and invite public scrutiny. Historically, Fair Trade Organizations (F.T.O.s) established trust relationships with consumers by emphasizing the direct partnerships that F.T.O.s had with the producers they represented in the marketplace. In the last two decades, certification conveyed through product labeling (see below) has emerged as a method of promoting certain Fair Trade standards.

Even more recently, F.T.O.s are creating new ways for consumers and producers to participate in information sharing. Larry's Beans, a member of the Fair Trade Federation and Cooperative Coffees, provides a documentation trail on its Web site consisting of actual receipts and invoices that allows visitors to see who was paid what along the value chain. Customers are encouraged to e-mail the Raleigh, North Carolina, operations with the lot number taken from a bag of Larry's Beans to get photos of audited documents related to the unique batch of coffee beans.

All members of the International Fair Trade Association, a global network of Fair Trade Organizations with members in seventy countries who believe that trade should improve the lives of marginalized people without harming the planet, must undergo a three-tier monitoring process to demonstrate accountability. The first step involves a self-assessment, including a survey of stakeholders. The second step consists of a peer review. Surveying their peers for feedback about business practices is a way for I.F.A.T. members to share information, promote high standards, and listen to producer perspectives. Results of the process are then used to create targets for improvement. Up to ten percent of I.F.A.T. participants also undergo a third step consisting of an external verification process that involves independent consultants. In 2004, I.F.A.T. launched the Fair Trade Organization Mark which recognizes members who successfully complete the monitoring process.

Long-term professional partnerships

Although the Fair Trade principles are an impressive and progressive collection, what makes Fair Trade truly unique is that its business operations are predicated on, enriched by, and sustained by direct and mutually beneficial relationships. Returning again to a value chain example, let's consider the case of a typical potter in Cuernavaca, Mexico. The potter and his or her family are skilled at mixing clay and creating plates and other pieces of dinnerware. They can mix the earth, shape

Figure 7 A Ten Thousand Villages staffer and partner from Bangladesh greet each other.

the clay, and dry the items in the sun. But they need help to get those products out of a saturated tourist market and into U.S. households, while securing enough steady income to meet their needs. They'll want technical assistance in determining what types of products will distinguish themselves in a demanding U.S. market. Several intermediaries are necessary. Working with a member of I.F.A.T., the potter's items can be analyzed and modified based on recent trends in consumer tastes. Once the pottery is finished, it will be packed and shipped from their cooperative to a Fair Trade wholesaler in the United States. That wholesaler will then sell the creations to a retail outlet that advertises to consumers of household accessories. The potters will hear about the consumers' reactions to their products – whether they were well-received or not and why – during a sales visit from the F.T.O. partner.

Because each participant along the chain transacts business according to Fair Trade principles with a commitment to improving the lives of producers, relationships are built and trust created. In fact, one of the requirements for Fair Trade wholesalers is to establish long-term contracts with producer groups so that the producers can be assured of a steady income. Multi-year agreements also strengthen connections and communications for the purposes of technical assistance. Not only do these partnerships reflect a more emotionally satisfying approach to handling business affairs, they also reap benefits, such as direct feedback channels for product development, personalized customer service, and responsiveness to issues along the supply chain. Fair Trade factors in human relationships as well as business practicalities.

Doug Dirks, public relations specialist for Ten Thousand Villages, explains the benefits of partnerships this way:

> If you come to shop in our stores, you can trust that we go to the trouble to get to know the people who made the products. Not everybody in every store knows every artisan, but as we go about our business everything we do is about the artisans. It is an interconnected chain and you can rely on us to promote equal relationships throughout the chain. Can you challenge your local hardware store to have the same chain? People have a responsibility to know the next person in the chain, and that person needs to know the next person. [It is important to] take care of the person next to you.

From the consumer perspective, Fair Trade partnerships mean that an individual can have a real connection with the person who crafted or harvested an object that is coming into the consumer's home. This connection may be as simple as the acquiring of unique, often one-of-a-kind products. After receiving a holiday gift pack of personal care products, one woman explained to me, "My bar of soap was signed by the woman who made it! I almost don't want to use it because the soap seems so special." This type of enthusiasm indicates a desire for products that are not cookie-cutter reproductions of mass produced items dictated by market research.

The freedom to enter into such partnerships and to embrace all the Fair Trade principles is a distinguishing feature of Fair Trade. The irony is that "free trade" policies are the ones most associated with choice and liberalization.

Should we look for the label?

As consumers make their choices, they need a marker or signal that helps them distinguish among products. The Fair Trade Certified™ seal is often residing on a supermarket shelf alongside similar products with labels indicating environmentally or socially responsible standards or membership in groups such as I.F.A.T. Some products boast more than one label. For example, a can of hot cocoa on my kitchen shelf distributed by Equal Exchange has symbols denoting Fair Trade, organic, and kosher certifications. Labels and fine print also inform me that the can was made of 100 percent recycled cardboard and that the distributor is a worker-owned cooperative. This array of labels can be confusing, but it is also an indicator of how awareness of social responsibility is entering the marketplace. Navigating through the labels can be made easier by familiarizing yourself with the different seals associated with food products. *What's the Deal with the Seal?*, created by Catholic Relief Services, is one overview that can be carried into a U.S. supermarket or retail outlet to help shoppers make educated, values-based decisions. It is also a great conversation starter with store employees. Dialogue with store owners lets them know customers are concerned about the sources of purchases and the conditions under which they are made.

In the Fair Trade world the Fairtrade Labeling Organizations International (F.L.O.) based in Bonn, Germany, establishes standards for Fair Trade certification, most usually of food. A network of independent national initiatives awards licenses to use a Fair Trade label on products based on F.LO. standards. F.L.O. itself certifies the producers of the products that ultimately bear a label on a retail product. The national initiatives are responsible for awarding licenses to companies whose products bear the retail label. The idea for a label to help consumers distinguish a product as Fair Trade came about in the 1980s through the work of Mexican farmers and a worker priest from the Netherlands. We'll hear more of that story in chapter five.

In the United States and Canada, the F.L.O. product label is administered by TransFair USA and TransFair Canada, respectively. The U.K. labeler is the Fairtrade Foundation. The Fair Trade Association of Australia and New Zealand handles certification for those countries. The F.L.O. associated label indicates that the product has been delivered to the marketplace after adherence to monitoring criteria and standards set out by F.L.O. "F.L.O. is one of the biggest international social economic certification bodies worldwide. It regularly inspects and certifies about 420 producer organizations in 50 countries in Africa, Asia and Latin America, embracing around 800,000 families of farmers and workers." Although labels are important signals on a particular product they don't tell the whole story of the company that brought the item to a store shelf.

Not all Fair Trade Certified™ labeled products are distributed by companies that adhere to Fair Trade principles in all business practices. Some mainstream businesses offer a wide selection of products that include limited Fair Trade options. Consumers can find, for example, Starbucks Fair Trade Certified™ coffee in coffee shops and "big box" stores, such as Costco. In 2005, McDonald's announced that it would be serving Green Mountain's Fair Trade Certified™ coffee in its restaurants located in the Northeast states in the United States. Nestlé, one of the world's largest purchasers of coffee worldwide, launched a Fair Trade brand for the United Kingdom market. This mainstreaming allows for a greater volume of Fair Trade products to be sold. In 2005, TransFair USA announced that 100 million pounds of Fair Trade Certified™ coffee had been imported into the United States alone since its beginnings in 1999.

With more labeled products on store shelves, consumer awareness of Fair Trade has also grown, but awareness can be a superficial state of mind. Some Fair Trade advocates worry that consumers may be ill-informed at best, or misled at worst, in thinking their purchase of a labeled product supports a Fair Trade organization totally committed to farmers and artisans. In reality the company may be embracing Fair Trade or other certification as a marketing tactic. This partial commitment reflects a major source of discontent in the Fair Trade movement. For some, mainstreaming trade is a way of reforming a broken system, instead of replacing it with a more just alternative. Bob Chase, chief executive officer and president of SERRV International, says:

> I think increasingly many people see Fair Trade as a way to "polish the rough edges of the capitalist system," to make the current system a bit more gentle. I think a move in this direction will result in the absorption of the movement into the mainstream capitalist system with little fundamental change in the global or local economies.

What's the Deal with the Seals? Adapted with permission from the CRS Fair Trade Program

This resource provides a side-by-side comparison of the logos you are most likely to find on your coffee and tells you what each one *really* does for farmers and the environment.

Fair Trade Certified

Name:
Fair Trade Certified
Certifying Agency:
TransFair USA, an affiliate of the Fairtrade Labelling Organizations

Fair Trade Federation

Name:
Fair Trade Federation
Membership Organization:
Fair Trade Federation

There are a lot of logos out there making a lot of claims about social and environmental responsibility. But Fair Trade is the only set of standards that guarantees farmers will earn a fair price for their coffee—enough to cover their costs of production and provide a worthy standard of living for their families.

The Fair Trade Federation logo pictured above at right is not a certification. It signifies membership in the Fair Trade Federation, an organization of wholesalers and retailers whose business models are built on Fair Trade principles.

 Smithsonian's Bird-Friendly Certification

Name: Certified Bird-Friendly
Certifying Agency: Smithsonian Migratory Bird Center

The Smithsonian's Bird-Friendly Certification process certifies that coffee bearing the logo above is grown under a dense forest canopy comprised of diverse species of trees. As its name indicates, the Smithsonian Migratory Bird Center is concerned primarily with the protection of the rare and endangered migratory birds that live in coffee growing regions.

 Rainforest Alliance Certified Coffee

Name: Rainforest Alliance Certified
Certifying Agency: Rainforest Alliance

Figure 8 What's the Deal with the Seals?

Rainforest Alliance Certification promotes the conservation of native ecosystems and forest protection by assuring compliance with a range of environmental, social and organizational standards.

 Certified Organic Coffee

Name: Certified Organic
Certifying Agency: United States Department of Agriculture (USDA)

Related Logos: In addition to the USDA logo above, your certified organic coffee may bear the seal of another USDA-accredited third-party certifying agency, such as those listed below.

- Quality Assurance International (QAI) Certified Organic— QAI is a private, independent, third-party organization that verifies producer compliance with the USDA's National Organic Program requirements.

- Organic Crop Improvement Association (OCIA)— OCIA is a non-profit organization that provides certification services to organic growers around the world.

- There are also state logos for certified organic products. Among the oldest and best known is the Oregon Tilth Certified Organic logo below.

As I will explain in chapter five, the history of Fair Trade is rooted in this alternative notion that the conventional ways of trading were unfair and should be changed on behalf of disadvantaged people. When multi-billion dollar companies such as Nestlé offer Fair Trade products concerns arise that Fair Trade is being co-opted and drawn away from its transformative aspirations on behalf of impoverished and disenfranchised people. For their part, many multinationals insist that adoption of Fair Trade or other socially responsible initiatives reflects a recognition that corporations must behave in accordance with internationally accepted norms of conduct.

Meanwhile, the use of the Fair Trade label has attracted controversy from both purists and the mainstream. A September 2006 *Financial Times* article unearthed alleged improprieties on coffee farms in Peru, claiming that Fair Trade cooperative members did not pay living wages to their hired labor. Mainstream companies may find these accusations particularly irksome because they cast doubt on a certification scheme that the businesses were reluctant to experiment with in the first place. The cycle of discontent continues as some fair traders have expressed dismay with how mainstream companies are attracted into licensing arrangements. Critics claim that in the pursuit of big volumes from reluctant corporations, F.L.O. initiatives are less rigorous in their monitoring of large licensees.

Taking the high road away from dissent within the movement, Bill Harris, director of Cooperative Coffees, points out that "[Fair Trade Organizations] help consumers look beyond labels to the commitment and practices of the enterprises that are producing a product. Product labels are, in my opinion, a stepping stone on the path to Fair Trade. You can certify transactions but fair trading relationships are much deeper." This focus on relationships is also of note when considering the handcrafted sectors, as those items – such as the greeting cards from Madagascar – are currently not eligible for certification because the great diversity of materials, products, and processes makes it much more difficult to standardize production practices.

The consumer decides

The purchasing of Fair Trade Certified™ products – whether from a mission-based Fair Trade Organization or a mainstream company –

undoubtedly helps grow the market for Fair Trade products. Researchers Low and Davenport note that the problem "implicit in building successful fair trade brands is that whilst mainstream retailers see the benefits of selling the products, they do not, with the exception of those "values-driven' retailers ... endorse the radical, transformative message of fair trade." This is born out in reality. As F.T.F. board member Dana Geffner of Pachamama World reports, "We are seeing applicants [for F.T.F. membership] that are using Fair Trade as a marketing tool rather than having a real commitment to Fair Trade. We have also been witnessing companies interested only in the Fair Trade criterion of paying the producers a living wage but not interested in the community development aspect of Fair Trade."

Partial commitment to Fair Trade may be an effort to "white-wash" business practices through an association with Fair Trade, or it may be a reflection of legitimate business concerns. McDonald's, for example, may be uncertain about the viability of specialty Fair Trade products in its fast food restaurants, which is why it is pilot testing the certified

Business Type	Engagement with Fair Trade Products	Engagement with Fair Trade Principles
	HIGHEST	**HIGHEST**
Fair Trade Organizations	Equal Exchange	_____
	Global Crafts	_____
Values-driven Organizations	The Body Shop	_____
	Green Mountain Coffee	_____
Pro-active Socially Responsible Businesses	Starbucks	_____
	Whole Foods	_____
Defensive Socially Responsible Businesses	Proctor & Gamble	_____
	Lowest	**Lowest**

Table 3. Business engagement with Fair Trade

coffee for one year in one region of the United States. Other businesses may have a sympathetic leaning toward Fair Trade principles within a certain business context. Although it offers a minimal number of Fair Trade Certified™ products, Starbucks insists that "Fair Trade Certified coffee is one part of a larger effort by Starbucks to be socially responsible in [its] relationships with coffee farmers and communities" and proudly notes that Starbucks is the largest purchaser of certified coffee in North America.

To summarize the array of businesses involved in Fair Trade, Canadian researchers Low and Davenport created a spectrum of retail businesses, ranging from total commitment to defensive acceptance. Using a modified version of the spectrum in table 2, I have placed the names of some companies as examples of "Engagement with products." I have purposely *not* assigned names in the column called "Engagement with Fair Trade Principles" as an invitation to the reader to assess businesses in their totality and make judgments as to their commitment to Fair Trade principles.

5

Fair Trade histories

Overview: the Fair Trade movement has a remarkable and multi-faceted history that is traced in this chapter. We will see how time and again the vision of ordinary people helped create and sustain key organizations and initiatives that put the concerns of small-scale producers at the center of their work.

Do you have any hobbies you are working on in your home right now? Maybe a home improvement project in your garage? Writing a blog on the computer in your office? Collecting clothing for the homeless in your spare bedroom? About a generation ago, Edna Ruth Byler, a church volunteer in Pennsylvania, got a little thing called the Fair Trade movement started in her basement.

Byler and her husband, J.N., worked with the Mennonite Central Committee, a relief, peace, and development organization of the North American Mennonite and Brethren in Christ Churches (M.C.C.). As part of their regular duties, the couple took a trip in 1946 to Puerto Rico, where Byler was introduced to impoverished seamstresses trying to improve their skills in sewing classes. The poverty the women were living in and the quality of their work inspired Byler to find a way to transfer their talent into income. Returning to her home in Pennsylvania, Byler began to sell the products to women in local sewing circles to help the Puerto Rican seamstresses work their way out of poverty. When she learned, through other M.C.C. connections, of products produced by Palestinian refugees in Jordan, she expanded the number of products she promoted.

Like many Fair Trade visionaries and practitioners, Byler volunteered her time and gave her money on behalf of her producer partners. Borrowing from friends and drawing from her own savings, Byler contributed more than $500 for her project. Over the course of several years, the popularity of the products grew and Byler became known as the "Needlework Lady," who sold products out of the trunk of her car. Between 1954 and 1958, Byler took orders from more than 2,440 individuals. Soon thereafter, Byler opened a gift shop in the basement of the home she and J.N. shared. After her husband's death in 1962, Byler's project was officially adopted by M.C.C., and she was hired as a part-time manager.

This project, which has flown under the banner of the Overseas Needlepoint and Crafts Project, and then SELFHELP Crafts, is now known throughout the United States and Canada as Ten Thousand Villages.

Was Edna Ruth Byler's first craft sale – which only brought in fifty cents – the start of the Fair Trade movement? Asking when the Fair Trade movement started is a little like asking who discovered America. Most U.S. schoolchildren are taught it was Christopher Columbus. But archaeological history shows that the Vikings visited North America hundreds of years before 1492. Indigenous people and anthropologists are likely to assert the continent was first explored a millennium ago. It all depends on your vantage point. So it goes with Fair Trade. There are so many different, and important, organizations and individuals who took part in the creation and have nurtured Fair Trade principles and practices, it is difficult to pinpoint one single moment in time.

I choose to highlight Edna Ruth Byler as a founder of the Fair Trade movement, not to dismiss the importance of parallel or closely related efforts, but because I believe that the single-minded, generous, and visionary commitment of individuals like Byler – whether they be leaders of non-governmental organizations, small business owners, development practitioners, or self-motivated volunteers – is what has made the evolution of Fair Trade possible and its future optimistic. Perhaps readers will see themselves in Edna Ruth Byler and will recognize that – whether through time, talent, or cold hard cash – they can shape the Fair Trade movement.

To consider the possible roles to play, let's look at the origins and operations of several key Fair Trade organizations in North America – known as the Fair Trade Four – as well as the proliferation of World Shops in Europe to trace Fair Trade's history. We'll also consider the early initiatives of producer groups, who infused grassroots perspectives into the model's development.

Ten Thousand Villages

From the trunk of Edna Ruth Byler's car to a retrofitted shoe warehouse in Akron, Pennsylvania, Ten Thousand Villages in the United States is now a multi-million dollar Fair Trade organization, having sold more than $20 million in fiscal year 2006 working with more than 100 artisan groups in thirty-two countries. In Canada, an independent Ten Thousand Villages thrives, working with 103 artisan groups in thirty-one countries. The name Ten Thousand Villages takes its inspiration from Mahatma Gandhi who said, "India is not to be found in its few cities but in the 700,000 villages … [W]e have hardly ever paused to inquire if these folks get sufficient [income] to eat and clothe themselves with." The mission of Ten Thousand Villages is to provide vital, fair income to Third World people by marketing their handicrafts and telling their stories in North America. The primary method by which Ten Thousand Villages reaches the consumer is a network of 160 store outlets. It also works with volunteers to host some 220 International Gift Festivals.

Perhaps because of its faith-based roots or the extremely direct trading between Byler and producers, Ten Thousand Villages has a history of cultivating deep and long-standing relationships with its overseas partners. Public relations specialist Doug Dirks explains the focus this way:

> Right from the beginning with Mrs. Byler, we met others who are less fortunate for one reason or the other. They have skills and we have money to spend. It seemed logical to take the need on one hand with the opportunity to help these people make a better living on the other hand and build an organization. That connection was the reason for our work from day one, it is the reason now and will be into the future.

Paul Myers, recent chief executive officer of Ten Thousand Villages and beloved counsel to many in the movement, emphasizes, "From the beginning, we've been interested in the grassroots and the small producer. We are concerned with ordinary people in small places who have limited opportunity. We believe "small is still beautiful.""

In order to operate "as a business with a compassionate mission by maintaining integrity in [its] actions and relationships," Ten Thousand Villages has codified the following principles:

1. We honor the value of seeking to bring justice and hope to the poor.
2. We trade with artisan groups who pay fair wages and demonstrate concern for their members' welfare.
3. We provide consistent purchases, advances and prompt final payments to artisans.
4. We increase market share in North America for fairly traded handicrafts.
5. We market quality products that are crafted by underemployed artisans.
6. We build sustainable operations using a variety of sales channels, including a network of stores with a common identity.
7. We choose handicrafts that reflect and reinforce rich cultural traditions, that are environmentally sensitive and which appeal to North American consumers.
8. We encourage North American customers to learn about fair trade and to appreciate artisans' cultural heritage and life circumstances with joy and respect.
9. We use resources carefully and value volunteers who work in our North American operations.

Myers describes the philosophy behind these operating principles as one approach to Fair Trade partnerships:

> [We] continue to work with a group as they strengthen themselves and their own efficiencies [in production]. We don't stop because they can survive without us as customers, but stay with them so they can help employ more people ...We have to be conscious about dependency and work on diversifying the customers to include some outside the Fair Trade community ... and, more and more, some local customers ... Producers say to us, "You provide the core of orders, so we can take risks with [mainstream businesses]."

Of course, these approaches and principles are only noteworthy if they translate into real action and activities. One Ten Thousand Villages

Figure 9 This artisan from Uganda Crafts is a partner of Ten Thousand Villages.

partner, Uganda Crafts 2000 Ltd., is an organization that works with disadvantaged artisans, who are disabled, widowed, or young. In addition to providing technical assistance, the organization also owns a retail store that provides employment to people with physical disabilities. Recently, Uganda Crafts was able to purchase an eighty-five acre plot of land where it plans to build a center for teaching youth with disabilities about income generation. Since 1995, Ten Thousand Villages has purchased baskets, placemats, hand-carved stools, and purses from Uganda Crafts. Betty Kinene, Uganda Crafts director, is quoted in a Ten Thousand Villages brochure as saying, "Ten Thousand Villages is doing a lot to improve the lives of many women in Uganda. When I look back over the years, many women came to Uganda Crafts with no hope for the future."

In addition to its producer partnerships, Ten Thousand Villages attributes much of its success and ethos to the use of dedicated volunteers.

Individuals like you dedicate some of their free time to work in Ten Thousand Villages stores greeting customers, stocking items, and telling the stories of Fair Trade success. Other volunteers commit to long-term placements at the Akron, Pennsylvania, headquarters taking on a variety of operational roles. Doug Dirks explains:

> We've worked really hard since at least 1985 to combine volunteer effort with a more professional effort. In our stores everybody has a paid full-time manager with professional training, and usually relevant experience. That's a great combination with our volunteers ... The volunteer is a connection to the community, who brings our store authenticity and spontaneity.

SERRV International

At another historic Fair Trade organization, SERRV International, based in Madison, Wisconsin, more than 4,000 volunteers donate their time and energy at the SERRV warehouse during the course of a year. During a visit there in 2006, I saw scores of volunteers – students doing community service, seniors donating time in retirement, people with learning difficulties gaining vocational skills – unpack SERRV inventory from approximately eighty-five artisan groups in some thirty-five different countries.

Much as Ten Thousand Villages, and in the same time period, SERRV started as a program of a faith-based organization, the Church of the Brethren, and later developed an alliance with Church World Service. SERRV, which stands for Sales Exchange for Refugee Rehabilitation and Vocation, began as an income generation project in 1949 through the sale of wooden cuckoo clocks carved by refugees in Germany. A significant portion of SERRV's present customers make purchases through programs of Catholic Relief Services and Lutheran World Relief. Bob Chase, chief executive officer, notes that although rooted in Christian faith, the goals of the SERRV founders were "to create a more just world, to reduce poverty, to offer an alternative to the prevailing economic system and culture [regardless of religion]." Nevertheless, the role of faith-based organizations in initiating and sustaining Fair Trade endeavors is not to be overlooked. In England, for example, the largest F.T.O. is Traidcraft, which began in 1979 as a Christian response to poverty. Numerous faith groups, such as the Jewish Fund for Justice, Presbyterian Church (U.S.A.), and the Unitarian Universalist Service Committee, are part of a broad American interfaith effort. In 1999, SERRV became an independent non-profit organization. While SERRV does operate two retail shops in the United States as well as selling Fair Trade products through printed catalogs, the Internet, and consignment sales under the name A Greater Gift, SERRV's role goes beyond the marketing of Fair Trade products. Cheryl Musch, director of international development, explains the innovative SERRV model:

> We are focused on capacity building … Our goal is to help producer groups become more independent by helping them get the training and tools they need to grow. In an ideal world, these groups would grow beyond SERRV, and could enter the commercial market, which is much larger than the Fair Trade market, in the future. Then we can move on to another group in greater need.

In 2006, SERRV gathered many of its East African producer partners for a training session on global market trends. The agenda covered practical topics, such as "Adding Value through Details and Packaging" and "The Value of Culture and Tradition in Product Development." Participant Joseph Muchina, the director of Trinity Jewellery Crafts in Kenya, said:

> I learned how to collect new ideas from the environment I live in by looking at the plants around me and collecting shapes from their leaves and colors from their flowers. I learned how to use the Internet to compare my products with the same kind that are being offered from all over the world, check their prices, quality, and presentation to give me a clue of what to correct if any [sic].

The incubator model adopted by SERRV reflects both its generation of experience as a Fair Trade leader and the development realities of the twenty-first century. As renowned European Fair Trade leader Carol Wills notes:

Illiterate or semi-literate men and women, without land, living in developing countries, have very limited choices in their lives. As their countries industrialize ... They are dependent on traditional knowledge and skills to meet their livelihood needs. They are also dependent on nontraditional markets to sell their products. Increasingly, the products they used to make for their own community consumption are being replaced with cheap, mass-manufactured items such as plastic buckets and sandals, power-loomed cloth and lightweight metal cooking pots.

Partnership with SERRV helps increase producer viability in the handcraft marketplace by offering the producers a place to sell their products and providing the time, space, and expertise they need to develop their organizations and options.

World Shops

Just as SERRV and Ten Thousand Villages grew out of post World War II efforts to help the disadvantaged and disaster survivors, humanitarian organizations, such as Oxfam, which was founded in the United Kingdom, were started to respond to and relieve suffering from famine and other causes. These organizations provided direct assistance relief services, such as the famous CARE packages distributed to war victims, and also eventually broadened their activities to promote long-term development. Researchers Low and Davenport explain that:

> Fair trade became part of the strategy for promoting development through the "Trade not Aid" philosophy first espoused by the U.N. Conference on Trade and Development in 1968. International aid was not considered a path to long-term development, with many arguing that the international trade system plays a pivotal role in creating and maintaining poverty in the South.

Reaching consumers with messages about the need for trade reform became a critical function in the Fair Trade movement. European stores originally referred to as Third World Shops began to sell crafts, build awareness, and mobilize citizens for trade campaigns. The first such World Shop was opened in 1969 in the Netherlands.

In 1994, the Network of European Worldshops, known by its punc-tuated acronym NEWS!, was established to initiate common campaigns across Europe with 2,500 shops as its base. This need for coordinated campaigns was a consequence of the creation of the European Union where fair traders could advocate together from a common platform. The first NEWS! "Food for Thought" campaign focused on the effects of trade liberalization on small-scale food producers, while the "Made in Dignity" campaign was concerned with labor conditions in the tex-tile industry.

The official information center for Slovakia's "Make Poverty History" campaign was housed in the TEN SENSES shop. Offering Fair Trade products and serving as a base of information about trade issues are el-ements of the typical model of World Shops, whether they are com-mercial enterprises or volunteer-run initiatives. In the case of TEN SENSES, the owner is Integra, a non-governmental organization in-volved in micro-enterprise work in Central and Eastern Europe.

In addition to pure advocacy, each year NEWS! organizes events to celebrate World Fair Trade Day, held the second Saturday of May. Every other year it convenes a conference for its 100,000 volunteers. I had the opportunity to attend a NEWS! conference in 2002, and that experience provided an important reference point for the Fair Trade Futures conference organized in the United States in 2005.

Equal Exchange

As the political agenda of the Fair Trade movement sharpened in the 1970s, food items – especially coffee – began to surface as important products for poverty reduction and political action. Responding to in-ternational peace and justice concerns with activism in their own com-munities, fair traders embodied the motto "Think Globally, Act Locally." Dutch advocates boycotted Angolan coffee while also orchestrating im-portation of Guatemalan coffee from Fair Trade sources in 1972. By the 1980s, some U.S. activists were protesting the Reagan embargo of Nicaragua by selling Nicaraguan coffee that had been shipped to the Netherlands, roasted and packaged, and then sent on to Canada. Reminiscent of Edna Ruth Byler selling embroidery from her trunk, activist Susan Redlich drove a car filled with Nicaraguan coffee from

Canada to Massachusetts. Members of the Northeast Cooperatives, who would later become founders of Equal Exchange, purchased the coffee and then sold it to solidarity organizations.

"The 1986 establishment of Equal Exchange was significant for its creation of a sustainable business model that produces a high-quality household product – coffee – while making a political statement." Over the course of twenty years, the company has proven that a for-profit enterprise can be 100 percent committed to Fair Trade and experience significant and sustained growth. Since 1990, Equal Exchange has had an average annual sales growth of twenty-four percent and shareholder dividends have averaged 5.17%. This success – enjoyed most significantly by its producer partners of coffee, tea, sugar, cocoa, and chocolate bars – can be traced to several elements of the Equal Exchange business model, including that it maintains a top-to-bottom pay ratio of three to one and that it is a worker-owned cooperative.

Rodney North, a long time Equal Exchange worker-owner, explains, "When [Equal Exchange] ... founders set out to create an enterprise that would maximize social contribution, not profits, they custom built Equal Exchange to support this mission – with attention to capital structure, bylaws, personnel policies, and so forth." After one year on the job, employees of Equal Exchange can become worker-owners and share the rights and responsibilities of a cooperative structure. Lynsey Miller, worker-owner since 2003, emphasizes, "Fair Trade requires farmers to organize themselves democratically and to promote participation and transparency. At Equal Exchange, we hold ourselves, as U.S. business people, to those same principles." It should be noted that in Scotland, the similarly named Equal Exchange Trading, is also a worker-owned cooperative with a commitment to distributing Organic and Fair Trade products in the independent natural food sector of the U.K. market.

Another innovation from Equal Exchange in the United States is its Interfaith Program, launched in 1996 in partnership with Lutheran World Relief (L.W.R.) and currently accounting for twenty to thirty percent of Equal Exchange's sales. A favorite joke among L.W.R. staff is that coffee is the "fourth sacrament," referring to its central place in Lutheran fellowship and community building. L.W.R., which is a relief and development organization working in thirty-five countries, helps believers across the United States transform a daily habit into a way to promote economic justice. In one year alone, Lutherans partaking in the 2003 "Pour Justice to the Brim" campaign more than doubled church purchases of Fair Trade coffee to a grand total of ninety-nine tons of Equal Exchange's coffee in one year.

Having recently celebrated its twentieth anniversary, Equal Exchange has continued its role of Fair Trade pioneer by marking that milestone with the participatory creation of a vision for the next twenty years of its history. At the Fair Trade Futures conference, Equal Exchange's co-directors facilitated a discussion with consumers and other Fair Trade organizations titled "Imagining Fair Trade in 2025." Although Equal Exchange seeks a world where all trade is conducted fairly, organizing director Virginia Berman points out, "The immense economic needs of disadvantaged producers will always be out there. Equal Exchange's mission will continue to be to help the producers under valid conditions for the family farmer."

MarketPlace: Handwork of India

In our historic review of the Fair Trade movement so far, we have recognized the important roles of trading organizations, but we shouldn't miss the fact that producers and their allies in the Global South established income generation projects that produced the products that were traded. Non-governmental organizations and socially motivated individuals helped establish Fair Trade organizations in the Global South to organize producers, provide social services, and facilitate exportation to the North through cooperative or other democratic structures. MarketPlace: Handwork of India is a prime example of a Fair Trade business that rose out of the needs of impoverished people to become an organization that fosters artisan employment and empowerment. MarketPlace's story shows yet again the impact individuals – like you, the reader – can make on the Fair Trade movement.

After earning a master's degree in the United States, Pushpika Freitas returned to her native India, where she worked as a social worker. In 1980, alongside her sister, Lalia Monteiro, and three slum dwellers in Mumbai, Freitas helped establish SHARE, a grassroots organization dedicated to helping women "earn a dignified living, reach their potential and redesign the destinies of their children." Soon thereafter, building on home-based sales in the Chicago area where she had studied, Freitas launched MarketPlace to lead sales and marketing activities for products created by Indian craftpersons who design and sew textiles. MarketPlace and SHARE work with fourteen cooperatives and small businesses managed by some 450 low-income women artisans in India. In the U.S., MarketPlace is the only Fair Trade organization that almost exclusively sells apparel.

When doing interviews for this book, I was regularly cautioned not to reduce Fair Trade to just a discussion of the price paid for a product. Looking at the MarketPlace success stories, it becomes clear that Fair Trade is about so much more than income generation. Shanti Singh, who is part of the Udaan Mandal Cooperative, reported to Freitas, "After attending the [cooperative's] training meetings for one year I have slowly started noticing some changes in myself. Now I have started

Figure 10 Pushpika Freitas sits among MarketPlace India artisans.

questioning myself: Where do I stand? What is my real status and identity in my house? Before I never would have even thought of things like this."

From her vantage point, Freitas explains it this way:

> Economic development is only the first step toward enhancing the self-esteem and leadership of the women artisans ... They are now using the skills they have developed in business to improve opportunities for their children and are also going one step further – they are influencing social change in their local communities, ensuring there is clean water, adequate daycare, and better health care facilities ... The women artisans are building a more concerned, liberated and enlightened next generation of both men and women. In the short term, their daughters are the immediate beneficiaries: they are completing high school, getting jobs and becoming involved in their futures, especially when and who they marry. The women are becoming strong role models in the eyes of their sons, which will influence their relationships as husbands and fathers in the future. Breaking the cycle of poverty is a long and arduous road and making women the central players in their families, communities and civic societies is a vital component of the process.

How the label began

The single most popular question I hear as a Fair Trade educator is some version of the question, "How do I know something is Fair Trade?" As we saw in chapter four, a label administered by the Fairtrade Labeling Organizations International (F.L.O.) is often used as a marker of Fair Trade products. Although the label has gained mainstream recognition in some 20 countries, the history of the label is a reflection of grassroots sensibility and empowerment. The story of the label is a story of Fair Trade partnerships between traders in the north and the south.

In the early 1980s, the Unión de Comunidades Indígenas de la Región del Istmo (U.C.I.R.I.), a large cooperative of smallholder coffee producers in Mexico, sought opportunities to sell directly to coffee buyers in industrialized countries. Father Franz Vanderhoff worked with the farmers of U.C.I.R.I., and used his connections in the Netherlands to help gain market access for the farmers. Vanderhoff explains, "We don't want charity; we want a just market … Justice in the marketplace, that means that the cost of production at least has to be paid … the farmer has a family, he has to have upkeep of the family so that has to be part of the cost of your product." In 1988, the Netherlands launched the first Fair Trade certification system, the Max Havelaar Foundation, naming the certification label after a fictional character in Dutch literature who was a champion of coffee farmers. The label was not only a way to help customers recognize a Fair Trade product but also an independent system to verify claims that a product was fairly traded. By the mid 1990s several country-based initiatives joined together to form F.L.O. as a certification umbrella mandated to apply and monitor Fair Trade standards worldwide. The United States was a market of particular interest.

At much the same time, the Institute for Agriculture and Trade Policy (I.A.T.P.), in the person of Guatemalan refugee Reginaldo Haslett-Marroquin, reached out to Mexican farmers to link their struggles to those of family farms in the heartland of the United States. One of those farmers, Luis Hernandez of the La Selva Cooperative, took conversations about the U.S. Farm Bill as an opportunity to convince I.A.T.P. to sell Fair Trade coffee. In addition to establishing its own Fair Trade coffee brand – Peace Coffee – I.A.T.P. also went on to conduct a series of meetings with pioneering Fair Traders to assess the need for an F.L.O. label in the U.S. market. After consultation with groups such as Oxfam, TransFair Germany, and Equal Exchange, I.A.T.P. decided to incorporate an F.L.O. initiative in the United States – TransFair USA.

By 1998, the organization was incorporated as a charity according to U.S. law and had convened a board of directors with start-up funding from the Ford Foundation. By mid-2006 TransFair USA certified more than 150 million pounds of Fair Trade coffee and had broadened its certification reach to include tea, cocoa, fresh fruit, rice, sugar and vanilla. The certifier to the north, TransFair Canada, also labels those products, except vanilla, as well as cereals such as quinoa, spices, cotton garments, wine, roses, and sports balls.

This divergence of product availability reflects efforts on the part of each F.L.O. initiative to balance the availability of goods from producers with the demand on the part of consumers as well as the interest of businesses to market Fair Trade products. This multi-stakeholder approach to product labeling is in the spirit of the partnerships that gave birth to Fair Trade Organizations.

The movement has come a long way from the trunk of a Mennonite woman's car. There have been some bumps along the road, inevitable pressures and strains in the evolution of a concept as it matures into a movement filled with a variety of institutions and outlooks. The perspective of consumers, taking their places alongside Edna Ruth Byler, the mythical Max Havelaar, and Shanti Singh, can only help advance the movement in its evolution.

6
Yes, but does it work?

Overview: there is no doubt that Fair Trade is growing, especially in terms of volume of sales worldwide. Behind the sales figures are more than five million producers and their families reaping the benefits of Fair Trade. This chapter looks at some of the real-life impacts of Fair Trade, particularly in Asia, and helps us explore the limitations of Fair Trade and some of the challenges the movement faces.

Does Fair Trade work? Savita Solanki of India thinks so:

My husband had a minor heart attack and he had to take different medicines at different times. Because of the Adult Education classes [at my cooperative], I could read the doctor's prescription and give him the right medication at the right time. He cannot read and he was quite impressed that I could.

(Pushpanjali Textile Cooperative)

Does Fair Trade work? Ashenafi Argaw of Ethiopia thinks so:

The marriage between fair trade and farmers has helped lessen the poverty for my people. Fair trade has saved the lives of poor farmers. And participating in fair trade requires that both buyers and growers are disciplined, honest, and fair.

(Sidama Coffee Farmers Cooperative Union)

Does Fair Trade work? Angelina Godoy of Seattle, Washington, thinks so:

I like the way Fair Trade connects daily consumption to issues of global injustice. I am a professor of Human Rights in Latin America. I have trouble helping students understand the relevance of what they learn. Fair Trade draws bridges explicitly. It is very empowering for consumers.

(Member of Fair Trade Puget Sound)

Testimonials like these are meaningful assessments of whether Fair Trade works because they provide real-life examples of how Fair Trade is transforming lives and communities. But numbers tell a good story, too. A survey, carried out in twenty-eight European countries plus North America and the Pacific Rim reported that global Fair Trade sales in 2007 reached a record figure of four billion dollars. The Fair Trade Federation's 2009 "Report on Trends in the North American Fair Trade Market" noted an increase in sales among American and Canadian Fair Trade Organizations of 106 percent between 2004 and 2006. When factoring in the growth of south-to-south trade among producer countries, the global Fair Trade market is inching towards $5 billion a year.

Nevertheless, a few billion dollars in trade is a drop in the proverbial global commerce bucket, and the real value of trading derives from the number of lives it helps improve. TransFair USA estimates that from 1998 to 2009 the value of additional coffee farmer income generated by Fair Trade coffee in the United States totaled $200 million for more than 219 farming groups.

Counting both artisans of crafts and growers of food, F.I.N.E. estimates that more than five million producers and their families in developing countries reap the benefits of Fair Trade. Although we have seen throughout this guide that the benefits of Fair Trade go far beyond price, the growth in sales is essential to reaching even more producers, and the Fair Trade marketplace seems to be growing robustly. In the United Kingdom, seventy percent of households were regularly buying at least one Fair Trade product in 2008. This was an increase from forty percent in 2007. Meanwhile, in the United States, TransFair USA estimates there are at least 40,000 retail outlets, such as supermarkets and coffee shops, offering Fair Trade certified foods.

Consumers are also beneficiaries through a variety of types of engagement. An estimated 100,000 Europeans volunteer their time and talent to promote Fair Trade. In the United States, there was a sixty-one percent increase in the number of staff and volunteers working in Fair Trade businesses in North America and the Pacific Rim in 2003. Angelina Godoy, who was quoted earlier, is among the number of people *not* counted in the FTF survey because her efforts take place in the context of promoting a Fair Trade coffee campaign that isn't affiliated with any particular business. When we factor in the number of consumers who have brought Fair Trade products into their home, we see that the reach of Fair Trade could also number in the millions.

With millions of different experiences of how, why, or if Fair Trade works, I turn our focus to one particular region, Asia, which accounts for forty-six percent of the value of Fair Trade products sold in North America and the Pacific Rim. With a wide array of jewelry, rugs, handcrafts, and gift items, Asia offers a stunning diversity of products and an impressive roster of producer groups. To obtain an even finer sense of impacts, let's start with perspectives from one country: India.

I confess to a troubled history with India. As an undergraduate exploring pacifism through Eastern religions, I was enamored of Mahatma Gandhi, whom I studied in sociology classes and encountered Hollywood-style through the eponymous Academy Award-winning film. When the opportunity to make my first international trip came in the package of a six-week study tour of India and Nepal, I signed up with little forethought of the economic realities of the subcontinent.

The extreme poverty – both urban and rural – the caste-based destitution that marred democratic aspirations, and the persistent discrimination of women horrified and repelled me. In a classic "ugly American" response, I returned from my immersion experience thinking India was a dirty, crowded, and hopeless place that only Mother Teresa could love. Two decades later, the fair traders of India have gently and persistently proved me wrong. As we saw in chapter five in the profile of Marketplace: Handwork of India, Fair Trade producers from that country are determined to use Fair Trade as a poverty alleviation strategy.

The Indian people have a rich tradition of cottage industries. During the country's struggle for independence, Gandhi pursued a revolutionary strategy of non-cooperation by promoting home-based production of clothing – called Khadi – thereby rejecting British products. This legacy of self-reliance and empowerment is reflected in the Tara (Trade Alternative Reform Action) Project formed in the 1970s. A study group at Jamia Millia University in Delhi wanted to make an impact on the lives of the "untouchables," or lower caste people, they encountered in the university's neighborhood. The group initially focused its efforts on helping home-based craftspeople refine and sell their products. Producers working with Tara receive training and advice related to production capacity, quality standards, and entry to local, regional, and international markets that were previously closed to them due to social status.

Its focus on empowerment and capacity building has led Tara to link its grassroots programs to broader international trade reform advocacy strategies, such as the Make Trade Fair campaign. It also uses its position to promote human rights, especially regarding child labor and the status of women. By addressing structural issues that impede artisan progress in the marketplace and in society, Tara "has become a leading voice in the movement." The linkage of economic, social, and political concerns means that the 1,000 associates of the Tara Project would also answer, "Yes, Fair Trade works."

It is important to recognize these success stories, not just to prove the point that Fair Trade works, but also to call attention to the fact that

Figure 11 A variety of cottage industries thrive throughout India.

small and medium-scale enterprises are viable and necessary options for many poor people. Asian economies are often portrayed in the media and by analysts as engines of manufacturing growth and the destination for information technology positions outsourced from the United States.

But, the reality for millions of Asians is that they live in remote locations without infrastructure and, especially in the case of women and girls, the benefits of schooling. Michael Sheridan, senior program advisor at Catholic Relief Services, notes:

> Fair Trade is responsive to local realities, and meeting the needs of producers within their context, in culturally sensitive ways. Fair Trade isn't opposed to economic modernization but it is concerned with meeting people where they are and giving them options ... It isn't a choice between sitting at a loom or at a desk at a software company.

Sheridan goes on to point out that, even when people do choose to leave their homes and communities in pursuit of less traditional work, they do so at the risk of cultural fragmentation and personal dislocation from families and social networks. In a study of Nepalese Fair Trade textile production, Rachel MacHenry identified lack of employment opportunities as the main reason men left their homes to work as drivers, laborers, road builders, trekking guides, and even soldiers, sending remittances back to their families. Nepalese women also sought cash as laborers or domestic servants or, in the case of girls, as prostitutes. MacHenry's study concludes that Fair Trade cooperatives offer an alternative to "limited, exploitative, and often dangerous employment possibilities" by utilizing traditional skills to improve livelihoods.

This term "livelihood" comes up often in the literature surrounding the impacts of Fair Trade. Development specialists recognize that to answer the question "Does Fair Trade – or any other anti-poverty strategy– work?" there must be a set of indicators to measure economic impact, producer organization growth, and personal development. These indicators taken together give a picture of livelihood, defined by the British Department for International Development (D.F.I.D.) as "the capabilities, assets (including both material and social resources) and activities required for a means of living." D.F.I.D., which has supported Fair Trade projects financially, has conceived an influential framework for sustainable livelihoods that:

> Attempts to identify the most pressing constraints faced by, and promising opportunities open to, people regardless of where (i.e. in which sector, geographical space or level, from the local through to the international) these occur. It builds upon people's own definitions of these constraints and opportunities and, where feasible, it then supports people to address/realise them.

Dr. Neela Mukherjee of Development Tracks in Research, Training and Consultancy is currently doing a study of Fair Trade and sustainable livelihoods in the state of West Bengal, India, in seven remote, indigenous villages characterized by poverty and social exclusion. Her holistic analysis considers social groups, type of housing, food security, property, coping mechanisms, health, education, and social status. Although final results are not available at the time of this writing, the research project gives a sense of the complexity of variables related to determining whether or not Fair Trade works for producers in their totality as human beings. True to the participatory emphasis of the livelihood framework, Mukherjee has already identified some supports that members of self-help groups have requested as they try to enter the Fair Trade marketplace: provision of work space; raw materials and market linkages; access to micro credit; training and education concerning quality; advertising; and, organizational development assistance to cooperatives.

Around the world, as the Fair Trade movement has grown and matured, academics and traders have focused more attention on such studies. In 2003, the European Fair Trade Association had a list of approximately thirty impact studies, primarily by organizations involved in direct trading. By 2005, the bibliography of the Fair Trade Resource Network had tabulated 200 entries of professional articles. Colorado State University evolved a research unit on Fair Trade coffee into the Center for Fair and Alternative Trade Studies. Consumers don't have to be scholars to gain access to the thinking and perspectives on the world of Fair Trade. The Internet has fostered virtual communities of inquiry, such as the Fair Trade and Ethical Consumption Workshop and the International Workshop on the Economics of Fair

Trade. Conferences, such as the Fair Trade Futures conference in North America, and symposia that are organized for celebrations, such as Fair Trade Fortnight in the United Kingdom, give consumers access to the debates and dialogue in the field.

The testimonials and profiles in this chapter and throughout this guide make the case that Fair Trade does make a positive difference. But, as is always the case in human endeavors, there are flaws and weaknesses. In my role as a Fair Trade educator, I often field questions and doubts related to the price received by producers, the surplus of Fair Trade products, and the concern that Fair Trade does not address the needs of developing countries adequately.

Journalists in particular have taken an interest in the price consumers pay for a Fair Trade product and how those dollars transfer to farmers. In "Fair Prices for Farmers: Simple Idea, Complex Reality," the *New York Times* reported that a British coffee shop chain added eighteen cents to the price of a Fair Trade cappuccino, although the chain had only paid a few extra cents for the beans. This type of price gouging is a limited, but unfortunate, consequence of mainstreaming, practiced by some companies that embrace Fair Trade as a marketing tool and not a business model. Consumers can be taken advantage of because they assume that the price they are paying is directly related to what the farmer received. Savvy shoppers need to compare costs of Fair Trade products and press companies about differences.

A related concern is that the fixed price for Fair Trade commodities does not meet the stated goal of covering the cost of production when considering inflation. The Fair Trade minimum price for coffee, now $1.25 a pound, did not change for almost a decade despite increases in the cost of production, which vary by region. Kevin Knox, a coffee consultant quoted in the *New York Times* article, notes, "In Brazil, $1.26 is a fortune ... In the forest in the mountains of Mexico, the money is barely enough to justify doing it." The members of Cooperative Coffees, a whole bean Fair Trade and organic coffee importer, in close consultation with their farmer partners, has recognized this type of variability. In 2005, the coffee buyers and the coffee farmers came together in Quetzaltenango or "Xela," Guatemala, and decided to raise their prices, independent of the certification system. The minimum floor price was increased from $1.21 to $1.25 a pound and the organic premium was raised from fifteen cents to twenty cents a pound. Effectively, this means that members of Cooperative Coffees are offering $1.30 and $1.50 a pound for Fair Trade and organic, respectively. For their part, farmers agreed to conduct a thorough survey of their current production and operating costs in order to inform future discussions about coffee pricings.

This type of initiative also addresses the reality that the guaranteed Fair Trade price is received by a Fair Trade cooperative, not the individual farmer. The misconception that a coffee farmer pockets a full $1.26 for each pound he or she sells is in some ways a reflection of how educators like myself tell the Fair Trade story. We try to compare market prices with farmer realities and use short-hand notions, such as "An impoverished farmer can receive as much as double the market price." More accurately, the farmer's cooperative receives the Fair Trade premiums. Cooperative structures are an essential feature of Fair Trade because they promote democratic decision-making and maximize resources for marginalized producers. It is highly unlikely that the Xela Accords would have been possible if individual farmers were taking their case one by one to coffee buyers. Cooperatives help farmers share knowledge and add extra leverage to negotiations. The cost of services that cooperatives provide farmers, such as training for quality improvement and managing exportation, are covered in part by the Fair Trade premium.

In the case of crafts, as we saw in chapter three, a price may be determined according to an hourly wage or a piece-rate and may be calculated according to the volume of a variety of products. Here, too, cooperatives and associations play an important role in helping the producer evaluate the product and get that product to market. June Nash refers to these organizations as "sales mediators" because they help make connections between isolated, impoverished producers and conscious consumers willing "to pay a fair price for the objects they buy that will take into account the needs of the producers and their families." These organizations, many of which function as non-profits, factor the cost of their mediation roles into the cost you, the consumer, pay.

In both food and craft sectors, not all producers who wish to be part of the Fair Trade system can access the market. There is a surplus of products made under Fair Trade conditions because the demand for those products is still limited. Although the statistics and trends we saw at the beginning of this chapter are encouraging, more consumers have to buy Fair Trade products in order to increase the sales volumes for producers. For example, Kuapa Kokoo, the cocoa cooperative profiled in chapter two, only sells two percent of its cocoa on Fair Trade terms. The rest of the cocoa must be sold at market prices, which may fluctuate well below the costs of production and offer no social premium.

Another dimension of this problem for growers of certified food products is that participation in the system depends on certain criteria, including requiring membership in a cooperative. As Professors Warning and Green have identified:

> The Fair Trade certification system emerged as a response to market and social-political conditions that marginalized small farmers ... [I]t is certain that some communities, whether because of the physical distribution of members, low social capital resulting from historical social and political circumstances, or other reasons will not be able to form cooperatives as is required for participation.

This type of exclusion is related to a larger concern that no matter how viable and appealing the Fair Trade model is, it is an insufficient mechanism to address the scope of poverty and marginalization around the world. As we noted at the outset of this guide, Fair Trade is not the solution to the problems of the poor; it is a solution that needs to stand alongside a variety of other approaches. Michael Sheridan of Catholic Relief Services notes:

> One of the great strengths of Fair Trade coffee is that it is structurally set up to serve small scale farmers, people on the margins of national economy and global economy ... [I]t is also a weakness in the sense that it precludes people worthy of concern – such as landless workers, workers on plantations – from participation. It is incumbent upon us to find approaches that meet the needs of those folks too. Part of Fair Trade's power and potential is its promise of poverty reduction. That is real because farmers own their farms. They are poor and marginalized but they do have their land. Fair Trade allows them to invest in that land and in social infrastructure to strengthen their communities. As development

practitioners we have to find more ways to do that and more ways for consumers to join those efforts.

Development practitioners, policy makers, and producers themselves are more likely to join in those efforts if they know consumers are interested in being part of a variety of solutions to poverty and discrimination. As readers put down this beginner's guide, they have the opportunity to pick up the cause of poverty reduction, to develop incomes in the Global South and to express values in the Global North.

7

Ordinary people making Fair Trade extraordinary

Overview: throughout the guide we've seen examples of individual initiatives that have shaped what Fair Trade is and how it works. This chapter takes a closer look at ordinary individuals and small institutions whose deep commitment and creativity serve as extraordinary role models for the movement.

The sheer diversity of characters makes it difficult to give proper attention to all the stories of inspiration, all the models of innovation, and all the levels of support dedicated to the Fair Trade movement. There are many stars on the stage and many supporting roles. The story of Fair Trade is infused with spirit and energy, sometimes sorely lacking in the more conventional realm of trade. Part of the power of Fair Trade lies in the individual hearts and minds that are attracted to its principles: people who create products, refine them, ship them, market them, sell them, and use them, all in the context of principled and long-term partnership. The movement becomes a collection of average individuals making modest contributions with far-reaching implications and setting high, people centered standards for their conduct and the results of their work.

I would like to shine the spotlight on some of these innovators and inspirations. Highlighting these specific stories in no way diminishes the work of millions of others contributing in ways seen and unseen. I offer these profiles to help sketch the picture of what Fair Trade is and can be, to encourage readers to emulate certain ideas and passions, and to create unique ways to make Fair Trade happen.

Fair Trade networker

The word "twin" conjures up the idea of sameness, of likeness, of equality. This makes the acronym of the Third World Information Network, a ground-breaking and visionary non-profit organization known for its commitment to treating producers as full partners quite appropriate and perhaps a bit prophetic. Twin, based in the United Kingdom, has spurred the establishment of producer-owned Fair Trade enterprises, moving the core principles of Fair Trade to a high bar of producer empowerment.

Twin was present at the creation of Cafédirect, the Day Chocolate Company, and AgroFair, three companies that have pioneered new approaches to traditional Fair Trade practices. Cafédirect was specifically created to place Fair Trade coffee on mainstream supermarket shelves and build a recognizable brand throughout the United Kingdom, thereby reaching beyond the alternative distribution mechanisms associated with faith and solidarity-based trade. Cafédirect is now the fourth largest roast and ground coffee brand in the U.K. As a trading company, Twin is responsible for the importation, logistics, blending, and quality control of the Cafédirect products, but sees itself not just as client of some twenty-six producer organizations but as a partner and friend.

A loyal friend, indeed, Twin used its own funds for working capital and bank guarantees for Kuapa Kokoo in its early years as a Ghanaian farmer association. Twin and Kuapa went on, alongside other partners, to form the Day Chocolate Company with a structure that provides for producer ownership, profit sharing and professional development. The implications of this model cannot be overestimated, because the Day Chocolate model not only builds markets for the farmers involved, it also helps those farmers shape the marketplace.

The European marketplace has an entire Fair Trade fruit bowl thanks to another Twin partnership, AgroFair. In the decade since 1996, Agro-Fair has successfully introduced bananas, mangoes, pineapples, oranges, lemons, and mandarins under the Oké brand in twelve European countries. Oké U.S.A. was launched in the United States in 2006, further extending the reach of a worker-owned innovation. Much like Day Chocolate, the fruit producers have a fifty percent interest in AgroFair, providing them decision-making power as well as a guaranteed customer for their products. Ecuadorian Fair Trade banana pioneer Jorge Ramírez sums up the model, "With AgroFair we get a fair price, a fair say and a fair share."

In each of these cases, Twin has undertaken these initiatives alongside other Fair Trade organizations, thereby strengthening cooperation and collaboration in the United Kingdom – a powerful marketplace for Fair Trade products – and offering up models for capitalizing on organizational strengths in the creation of new trading structures.

Doing so was not always easy. In the beginning, the staff of Twin numbered no more than six and the organization existed with very little capital. In the eighteen months it took to get the first package of Cafédirect onto supermarket shelves, farmers had to wait for payment. Consumers did their part, too. In the absence of high-priced advertising campaigns, the word was spread for consumers to stuff customer service boxes with demands for Cafédirect. Twin's former director, Pauline Tiffen, characterized Twin's innovations as downright daring. "We punched way above our weight as the boxing metaphor has it, until it became true. The same is true for Divine. We dreamed big, worked hard until it all happened."

Twin's attitude, its intelligence, and its commitment to collaboration ensure that it lives up to the "N" in its name, as a network of diverse partnerships and linkages across the world. Robin Murray, chair of Twin's board, says that a remaining challenge for pioneers like Twin is to "ensure they remain innovators, that they operate according to a "gold standard' of Fair Trade and that their message is not diluted."

Fair Trade maverick

"If someone discovers Fair Trade through me and then goes to a competitor, so be it. My job is to hook them – that's all." Those words might not sound fitting coming from a former economics major, but Larry Larson, founder of Larry's Beans, is known for defying expectations and pursuing a savvy, but farmer-friendly, business model. Larry's Beans enjoyed 300 percent growth in just three years by combining edgy, tongue-in-cheek branding efforts with heartfelt commitment to Fair Trade principles. It doesn't seem like he is losing much business to the competition.

Originally from Seattle, Washington, Larson admits that he started out as a coffee geek, obsessed with the finer elements of roasting and brewing coffee. He searched the world looking for the perfect beans to create, as the company's website proclaims "supremely delicious coffee." It wasn't until he met farmers in Chiapas, Mexico, that Larson transformed into a self-proclaimed Fair Trade maverick, who put the concerns of his producer partners and the environment they worked in at the forefront of his concerns. "After I met farmers in the highlands of Chiapas, saw their commitment to the land, saw the incredible impact Fair Trade was having on their families and communities, just selling great tasting coffee wasn't sufficient," Larson reports.

Larson has created a distinctive brand as a way of selling the farmers' beans and introducing his customers to the principles of Fair Trade and sustainability. Larry's packages feature cartoon characters and names, such as Frank Sumatra and Bean Martin, that defy you not to pick them up. His Web site offers sweatshop-free underwear and coffee gadgets for sale, as well as a CD offering the folk music of Nicaraguan farmers, with all profits returning to Nicaragua. These marketing efforts and product offerings have captured clients large and small, ranging from intimate coffee houses in North Carolina to the international headquarters of Catholic Relief Services. But being a successful businessperson is not enough for Larson. Seeing his business as a manifestation of his personal philosophy, Larson wants to help introduce consumers to the range of possibilities for creating a better world.

One example is the Larry's Beans delivery truck, fueled by recycled vegetable oil. "With a snazzy blue and brown paint job with loads of information about Fair Trade, Organic, Shade-Grown coffee, the "veggie" bus attracts stares, questions and occasional whoops of support wherever it goes." Even if you don't live in the local delivery area, Larry's Bean's "Sustainability School" provides links and information on topics, such as water conservation and animal companions. Larson explains:

> I really believe we all have to decide the type and depth of our commitments. I want to help my customers discover what is important to them. I think Fair Trade, recycling, animal rights, organics, these are all compelling causes, but I can't tell anybody else what is important. You have to discover that on your own. I'm happy to fuel your journey with great coffee and some helpful suggestions.

Fair Trade communicator

If there were an award for best tag lines in the world of international development and relief organizations, Oxfam would win it. The organization managed to distill a comprehensive strategy of political activism, consumer engagement, and corporate pressure into the simple "Make Trade Fair" slogan with its ubiquitous lime green equal sign. An oft-quoted and influential policy paper by Oxfam revealed some of the best thinking and most useful strategies for reforming international trade and was memorably dubbed *Rigged Rules and Double Standards*. Oxfam has a well deserved reputation for creating incisive, hip, and appealing campaign and educational materials.

Oxfam America, a member of Oxfam International, has mastered the art of grabbing consumer attention, providing informative and accessible material, and offering specific, and often enjoyable, ways to become involved in Fair Trade. Katherine Daniels, trade policy advisor, explains that Oxfam tries to meet people where they are and help them identify issues of interest so that individuals can develop passion for those issues. One of the first efforts at Fair Trade work in the U.S. occurred when Oxfam provided a grant to Equal Exchange to buy its first shipment of El Salvadoran coffee some twenty years ago. Oxfam Great Britain, however, has been involved in Fair Trade since its early days. Oxfam Trading was established in 1964 as the first British Fair Trade organization.

LARRY'S SUGGESTIONS TO VOTE WITH YOUR DOLLARS AND GET MORE FOR YOUR MONEY!

Use recycled materials: Landfills create toxins. Recycling creates jobs and new industries.

Buy energy-efficient products: Reduce pollutants and global warming emissions from power plants, plus save money.

Buy local: Keep jobs and money in your community.

Buy organic: Tastes delicious. Reduces pesticides in our soil, our water, our children.

Buy Fair Trade: So you know a fair price was paid to the producer.

Buy American: Stop companies from outsourcing.

Ask questions: Stay informed.

Coffee became a focus of the Make Trade Fair campaign in 2002 when the price of coffee dipped to a thirty-year low, affecting millions of small farmers who depend on cash income to pay for food, school fees and health care. Oxfam reacted in a variety of ways to educate consumers, pressure companies, support farmers, and change policy. It also recruited high profile celebrities, such as the band Coldplay, to its cause.

In the United States, Oxfam's commitment to training college students has created a base of politicized, informed young people, who began demanding Fair Trade on their campuses and eventually formed the United Students for Fair Trade (see chapter eight).

The advocacy work Oxfam does is critical because it addresses the life and death issues faced by its partners in a way that creates options for consumers like you to get involved. That involvement, as we have seen throughout this book, has direct impact on the lives of the disadvantaged and can also animate our own lives for the better. Two key Oxfam coffee program staff members are emblematic of how Fair Trade commitments relate directly to personal values.

Seth Petchers, coffee program director, returned from a year-long exposure to poverty in Asia determined to translate his concern for the social and environmental consequences of globalization into advocacy for Fair Trade. The inspiration of individual coffee farmers infuses Petchers' work. He related to me the story of Don Antonio Cavajay Ixtamer, a Guatemalan farmer whose land was devastated by a hurricane just when the worst of the coffee crisis was subsiding. When Petchers asked if the farmer would be able to salvage the land, Ixtamer said, without hesitation, "*Si se puede*" or "Yes, we can."

Shayna Harris, who works alongside Petchers in the Oxfam coffee program, also finds the stories of producers to be an essential force in her work. She decided to take a trip to Mexico to live among struggling farmers and learn how Fair Trade affected their families and communities. Now Harris says, "To work for Fair Trade is to return the favor of hospitality of the people I lived with in Mexico. I can share their love, their culture, and their story. When I asked them at the end of my visit, "What can I do that is useful to return the favor?' they said, "Talk about us.' "

Don't let the catchy phrases and the celebrity endorsements of Oxfam intimidate you. Sharing stories and spreading the word about Fair Trade is the essence of Fair Trade communication.

Fair Trade instigator

In *The Tipping Point: How Little Things Can Make a Big Difference,* Malcolm Gladwell identifies key factors involved in creating "social epidemics" or large shifts in behavior among a critical number of people. Central to successful social epidemics are individuals – connectors, mavens, and salespeople – who possess particular traits, such as deep expertise in subject matter or a vast number of personal contacts. Stephanie Sheerin defies a tidy Gladwell categorization, but she is clearly someone who wants other consumers to catch the Fair Trade bug.

First, there is Sheerin's relentless drive to incorporate Fair Trade into her daily life. She was first exposed to Fair Trade when she stumbled upon a small, independent store and the owner explained the Fair Trade mission. Sheerin immediately switched her daily cup of hot tea to Fair Trade and adopted a new eating habit through Fair Trade chocolate. Then, as the holiday season approached, Sheerin wrote to her family and friends encouraging them to give Fair Trade gifts and pointing them in the direction of Fair Trade companies.

Hungry for information as she tried to spread the Fair Trade message, Sheerin joined Global Exchange, an international human rights organization dedicated to promoting social, economic, and environmental justice around the world. Global Exchange campaigns and action alerts were easy for her to respond to and easy to pass on. She joined a number of other organizations for background information and organizing ideas. If Sheerin is not a card-carrying member of every socially responsible advocacy group there is, she at least knows how to access its resources.

But, Sheerin isn't just a joiner; she's a leader, too. She creates appealing community activities and rolls them out at places like farmers' markets, yoga studios, and Fair Trade stores. Sheerin organized sales at a local United Church of Christ during the 2005 holiday season and sold $18,000 worth of Fair Trade merchandise, donating $5,000 in profits to Hurricane Katrina relief efforts.

I have been shoulder-to-shoulder with Sheerin at public events and always come away astounded by her energy and commitment. When I asked her how and why she is so involved in Fair Trade, Sheerin explained. "People want this. They want to live their lives consistently .... most people want an option that is more consistent with their values and is social justice oriented and is respectful. There is an endless pool of people that will support Fair Trade once they learn about it and that sustains me."

Fair Trade peacemaker

Being a coffee farmer is demanding work, as you aim to produce at least 1,000 of the right beans for one pound of coffee. Planting, tending, composting, and harvesting are even more difficult if a decades-old civil war simmers around you. Such is the reality of COSURCA – Empresa Cooperativa del Sur del Cauca – which is a 1,700 member farmers' cooperative located in the south of Colombia, South America, where a low-intensity war first began in the mid-1960s. The mission of COSURCA, much like other Fair Trade cooperatives, includes improving crop quality, promoting market access, and enhancing the social and economic conditions of its members. The odds are stacked against the cooperative, though, as it draws the attention of armed extremist groups, who value the region for its proximity to the jungle and natural resources.

COSURCA's soft-spoken but fiery manager, René Ausecha Chaux, sees one of his primary roles as reinforcing for farmers the benefits of cooperative membership. "A very important issue for us is the ability to produce our own food in times of war. If we produce a lot of grain, fruit, and vegetables that can be stored, we prevent our people from having to leave and abandon the land. It is this chance at life that allows us to live through a war that has lasted forty years."

Nevertheless, members of the cooperative are sometimes tempted to shift production from coffee to coca, which is a much more lucrative, if illegal, crop sought after by warring factions and drug dealers. Although Fair Trade prices can't compete with illegal payments, Ausecha Chaux persists in making the case that the cooperative creates additional benefits beyond cash, such as establishing a food security fund for home consumption and creating a composting program. Ausecha Chaux emphasizes, "So many farmers have had to choose between growing illegal crops like coca or facing poverty for themselves and their families. With the right resources at their disposal, coffee cultivation offers them a viable, safe option."

It is a cruel irony that some of the resources invested in COSURCA by the U.S. Agency for International Development were decimated by the clearance efforts of Plan Colombia, a U.S. government project that attempts to eradicate coca production through aerial spraying with herbicide. In May and June of 2005, fifty-seven COSURCA families, "watched in horror as crop-duster planes dropped white clouds of herbicide onto their farms," effectively destroying their organic certification and the price premiums associated with it. COSURCA estimates that $13,000 worth of coffee was lost to the cooperative because of the mistaken spraying exercise.

I have not been able to speak to Ausecha Chaux since the spraying, but I can imagine his response. His eyes would be sad and his voice quiet; but, his faith in the farmers and in his Fair Trade partners would be resolute. He believes in Fair Trade because he has seen its impacts prevail against frightening and life threatening challenges.

We see in these profiles individuals and innovators who have brought the best of their vision and skills to making connections, empowering producers, activating citizens, and spreading the Fair Trade message. They all believe in the potential of Fair Trade. To create a sustainable Fair Trade movement will require more ordinary people joining them and making their own unique contributions.

8

Will free trade ever be fair?

Overview: trade agreements and international institutions, such as the World Trade Organization, have exerted enormous influence around the globe. Using recent examples of trade events, this chapter helps us understand the power we have as citizens to demand agreements that reflect the same principles that characterize the Fair Trade system.

We've seen that the dollar – pound or Euro – is an economic ballot. Thoughtful decision making about how consumers spend their money affects the lives of farmers and artisans struggling to improve their livelihoods. Every purchase is also a mini-referendum on the company behind the product or service. Consumers cast currency ballots and vote for the companies that reflect the values and principles they believe in. This power cannot be dismissed as we trace the enormous boom in socially responsible business, resulting in part from the success of consumer advocates pressuring companies to change their practices. More and more policy makers and thinkers across the political spectrum are recognizing this power. Former staff economist at the General Agreement on Tariffs and Trade, now the World Trade Organization, Edmund J. Sheehey, notes, "Seemingly small differences in our purchases make enormous differences to poor producers and can send powerful messages to corporations about their labor and environmental practices ... The Fair Trade movement helps the producers involved and puts real pressure on other producers, including multinational corporations, to improve their practices."

But voting power does not start with behavior at the store. In the Global North most consumers have actual voting rights as citizens and have the freedom to choose the politicians who enact free trade agreements among countries. Many readers may be wondering why anybody would ever be against something called "free." Especially in democracies, such as Canada, the United Kingdom and the United States, freedom is cherished and promoted. In another irony of language, in the case of international trade, "free" can mean that some governments are free from trade restrictions. Because most trade is actually conducted by businesses, this means corporations are free to behave in ways that are harmful or predatory. In a commentary in the classic *Small Is Beautiful: Economics as If People Mattered*, Helena Norberg-Hodge points out, "It is in robust, local-scale economies that we find genuinely "free markets'; free of corporate manipulation, hidden subsidies, waste, and immense promotional costs that characterize today's global market."

An excellent example of free trade rules run amuck is a case documented by the Mexican Free Trade Action Network and Tufts University's Global Development and Environment Institute. In 1993, U.S. multinational Metalclad Corporation purchased a toxic-waste company in the state of San Luís Potosí, Mexico, where it planned to reopen a hazardous waste dump. When the local community protested and the municipal officials rejected Metalclad's plans, the corporation filed suit under the Chapter 11 provision of the North American Free Trade Agreement. Metalclad claimed that government actions taken to protect citizen health discriminated against it as a foreign firm. The government of Mexico ultimately had to pay the corporation a $15 million fine when two arbitration panels ruled against the country and its citizens. "The case has become one of the leading examples of the way Chapter 11 undermines local rights, national sovereignty, and governments' ability to regulate the activities of private companies to protect health and the environment."

These trade agreements have far-reaching impacts on developing countries, as governments pursue reduction of trade barriers and easier mechanisms for foreign investment. In response, there are a variety of interrelated campaigns and coalitions at the national and international levels that seek to restructure and reform the trade systems and structures that are, according to Katherine Daniels, trade policy advisor for Oxfam America, "keeping people poor."

The effectiveness of anti-poverty campaigns was demonstrated by the gains resulting from the debt relief – or "Jubilee" – campaigns. Taking "Jubilee" from the biblical injunction that every fiftieth year "those enslaved because of debts are freed, lands lost because of debt are returned, and community torn by inequality is restored," an alliance of justice activists has pressured international organizations to reduce or eliminate the burdensome debt of developing countries. In 2005, the Group of Eight Industrialized Countries (G8) – Canada, France, Germany, Italy, Japan, Russia, the United Kingdom, and the United States – agreed to cancel the debts of approximately twenty countries considered to be heavily indebted. Often incurred by corrupt or dictatorial governments, these obligations siphoned funds from anti-poverty initiatives in needy countries. Although Jubilee advocates considered the G8 relief an important precedent, they view it as only an initial step toward cancellation of all unjust and unpayable debts.

All the interrelated campaign concerns help citizens like you to confront the complex problems of poverty through the political ballot. The micro level principles of Fair Trade, such as providing living wages, protecting the environment, and promoting democracy, come to bear on the macro level considerations of government trade agreements and the role of multinational corporations. Citizens need to monitor these agreements but their intricacies and acronyms can be confusing. See the appendix for guidance on some of the key terms and campaigns. United for a Fair Economy neatly spells out the role and reach that trade agreements have.

Chapter two compared how conventional or free trade differed from Fair Trade in the micro context of profit motives and operational practices of businesses, but with international trade valued at $10 million each minute, on the world stage these differences are more stark and their implications more dangerous.

The seminal *Rigged Rules and Double Standards* sums the situation up:

> While rich countries keep their markets closed, poor countries have been pressurized by the International Monetary Fund and World Bank to open their markets at breakneck speed, often with damaging consequences for poor communities ... Meanwhile, powerful transnational companies have been left free to engage in investment and employment practices which contribute to poverty and insecurity, unencumbered by anything other than weak voluntary guidelines ... The WTO's bias in favor of the self-interest of rich countries and big corporations raises fundamental questions about its legitimacy.

These questions of legitimacy first garnered worldwide attention through the demonstrations accompanying the 1999 meetings of the

World Trade Organization (W.T.O.) in Seattle. The W.T.O. had been formed only a few years earlier as "the only international organization dealing with the global rules of trade between nations. Its main function is to ensure that trade flows as smoothly, predictably and freely as possible." In Seattle, protestors representing labor and environmental interests protested against unrestrained free trade. At the same time, trade ministers from African countries refused to negotiate because of their discontent with one-sided deals.

With the N.A.F.T.A. free trade legacy lingering and concerns about the unequal power structures within W.T.O. remaining, the 2001 Doha Declaration, named for the location of the W.T.O. negotiations, promised a greater focus on development concerns. Recognizing that the majority of W.T.O. members are developing countries, the ratifying countries stated the following intentions:

> [T]o place their needs and interests at the heart of the [declaration's workplan] ... we shall continue to make positive efforts designed to ensure that developing countries, and especially the least-developed among them, secure a share in the growth of world trade commensurate with the needs of their economic development. In this context, enhanced market access, balanced rules, and well targeted, sustainably financed technical assistance and capacity-building programmes have important roles to play.

The next round of negotiations in 2003 in Cancun reflected major discontent with the progress made toward those intentions. Structural problems with the W.T.O. remained as developing countries had the deck stacked against them in terms of capacity to go toe-to-toe in negotiations with the United States and European Union. The E.U. and U.S. arrived in Cancun with 800 negotiators each. The African country of Nigeria, on the other hand, had twelve negotiators, who were often expected to cover all aspects of the almost round-the-clock proceedings. Governments come to negotiations to promote the interests of their individual and corporate citizens. Again, developing countries were often outnumbered considering that the U.S. based Wal-Mart had profits exceeding the economies of Ghana and Mozambique combined.

Civil society – the term used for organizations and individuals who do not represent corporate or government institutions – rallied in full,

EXCERPTS FROM OPEN LETTER TO GOVERNMENTS REGARDING FAIR TRADE, SEPTEMBER 2003

On the occasion of the WTO Cancun Ministerial, we, members of the international Fair Trade movement, call on governments and international institutions to contribute to the expansion of Fair Trade and the promotion of a global trading system that truly works for poverty reduction and sustainable development. We offer the following concrete proposals ...

Trade policy should not promote and enforce liberalization as an economic solution where "one size fits all."
Trade policy should be made in a fair, transparent and democratic way, seeking the full participation of the small and medium-sized enterprise and agricultural sector in developing countries.
Trade policies should promote an enabling environment for Fair Trade that upholds the right of producers and consumers to take part in Fair Trading without restriction.

diverse force to provide alternatives to free trade dogma and dominance. Fair traders used the proceedings to make the case that "people and the environment [should be] at the heart" of the world trading regime.

I had the opportunity to participate in a Fair Trade Fair and Sustainable Trade Symposium, organized by a consortium of trade advocates, parallel to the official activities. A retail mall in Cancun was transformed into a Fair Trade marketplace featuring products from twenty countries. The producers in attendance gave tangible evidence of the viability of Fair Trade. A forum of workshops and panel discussions drew hundreds of advocates, producers, businesspeople, and government representatives determined to infuse the W.T.O. events with Fair Trade sensibilities. Fifty groups signed a Letter to Governments that offered a series of policy recommendations.

In the end, the Cancun negotiations broke down when a block of developing countries remained firm in its resolve to not allow the addition of new trading issues to the agenda until development issues had been resolved. A variety of trade justice, *campesino*, indigenous, and anti-globalization groups claimed a central role in this victory. Yet, the victory for developing countries and civil society was bittersweet. The collapse of negotiations signaled no forward movement on issues of critical concern. Further, the United States trade representative used the breakdown in negotiations as a pretext to adopt a new strategy of negotiating bilateral and regional trade agreements. Oxfam America's Katherine Daniels characterized the shift as reflecting an "imperial mindset" of what America can and cannot do with its liberalization agenda. Trade representative Robert Zollick uttered a sound bite characterizing developing countries as either "Can Do" countries or "Won't Do," with the implication that "Can Do" countries would be favored in a range of U.S. policy decisions.

This new approach to negotiating regional free trade agreements, at least on the part of the United States, is a call to action for citizens to continue their trade justice advocacy. While not all the outcomes are universally praised by fair traders, citizens are demonstrating an ability to make a difference. One of the first major regional agreements taken up by the United States after N.A.F.T.A., the Free Trade Area of the Americas (F.T.A.A.), has been sidelined through the efforts of citizen groups.

Built on the same premise as N.A.F.T.A. and the Central America Free Trade Agreement (C.A.F.T.A.), F.T.A.A. would extend many of the same troublesome aspects of free trade to South America, such as the weakening of labor rights and the "race to the bottom" in low-wage countries, dilution of environmental laws, privatizing of water and other essential public services, and shifting decision-making from the public sphere to non-democratic tribunals and arbiters. The environment for most bilateral or regional agreements is also detrimental to developing countries because the regions do not have the power, leverage, size, or economies to compete with the United States.

The deadline for U.S. ratification of F.T.A.A. was January 2005, but as of this writing, no deal has been reached. The Doha rounds of the W.T.O. are considered dead, with no significant progress made in negotiating agreements acceptable to both the Global North and South. These developments can be attributed in part to the mobilization of ordinary citizens in both hemispheres. Approximately 10,000 people gathered in Miami in November 2003 to protest the F.T.A.A. Ministerial.

Many of these people were affiliated with the Hemispheric Social Alliance (H.S.A.), a coordinator of actions, campaigns, and strategy meetings. Similar to the global Trade Justice Movement, the H.S.A. is formed from national and regional coalitions. "The backbone of these movements in many Latin American countries [is] the Indigenous peoples and farmers ... whose entire way of life is threatened by the proposed F.T.A.A." The fate of W.T.O. negotiations and free trade agreements is clearly shaped by consumers and producers coming together, not only in physical spaces like Cancun, Doha, and Miami, but also philosophically and politically to work for trade justice.

Fair Trade identifies consumers as being a central force in "supporting producers, awareness raising, and in campaigning for changes in the rules and practice of conventional *international* trade." (emphasis mine) But there are also local opportunities to shape Fair Trade domestically.

Figure 12 Small farmers in the United States are finding ways to promote domestic Fair Trade in their communities.

Responding to the decrease of family farms and the corporate control of factory farms, Family Farm Defenders in the heartland of the United States is working to apply principles of economic justice at home. In addition to political advocacy and programs such as North-South farmer exchanges, Family Farm Defenders is supporting a cheese project in Wisconsin. Selling Fair Trade cheese is a way to educate consumers while offering healthy, nutritious and fairly priced cheese.

Moving south in the United States, the Federation of Southern Cooperatives, a technical assistance and advocacy group of African American farmers, has developed a partnership with Red Tomato to market watermelons in the Northeast. The United Students for Fair Trade participated in the boycott that pressured PepsiCo to increase payment to migrant farmworkers who harvested tomatoes sold in Taco Bell restaurants. Wisconsin farmer John Peck says, "For family farmers who believe in stewarding the land, respecting animals, providing healthy, wholesome, nutritious food, and building an equitable democratic society [Fair Trade] just makes common sense."

Another commonsense direction for Fair Trade, particularly as it relates to trade policy with other countries, is to dismantle race disparities in the currently predominantly white movement. As the movement succeeds in changing the terms of trade, it needs the experience and wisdom of first and second generation immigrants to industrialized countries, alongside other people of color, as key informants of trade debates. Fair Trade holds the promise of being a bridge builder between advocates for fairer trade, whether it be domestic or international.

9

The future of Fair Trade

Overview: throughout this guide, we have explored Fair Trade as a form of capitalism with a conscience that allows consumers to be truly free to participate in a system that upholds their values. There are a variety of ways consumers can choose to participate in Fair Trade, and at deeper levels of involvement they are likely to encounter some of the tensions and difficult issues the movement faces. This chapter sets out some of those challenges and offers questions for the reader to consider in shaping the future of Fair Trade.

I started this guide with a memory of the 2005 Fair Trade Futures conference, a gathering of 750 people from twenty countries who were interested in what Fair Trade could mean to them, their families, and communities of the world into the future. The conference was conceived for many reasons, not least of which was the need for a time and place to contemplate the emerging challenges and potential fault lines in the movement. The issues arising from the success of Fair Trade are sometimes complicated and not easily resolved, reflecting the complexities of our world today and, "the blurring of previous boundaries between the economic sphere and the political, social, and cultural realms" of our lives as consumers.

The organizers of the Fair Trade Futures conference were interested in how "Living a Fair Trade Life" meant achieving social justice and change through the market. They – myself included – wanted to create the chance for individuals whose life values and personal vision match those of Fair Trade to build and deepen the vision of the Fair Trade movement. We also welcomed mainstream companies with only a limited offering of Fair Trade products. As is the case in most efforts for social and economic justice, there is a tension between "revolutionaries" and "reformers." In the Fair Trade movement boundaries have sometime been drawn between "100 percenters" and "mainstreamers," or between "for profit" and "non-profit" organizations.

Into the future, diversity could be an asset to the movement. The complexities and controversies of Fair Trade reveal the vibrancy of the movement. As Valerie Orth of Global Exchange notes, "People are constantly questioning Fair Trade. Infighting isn't good but pushing each other is. Fair Trade can be confusing: Are we marketers or are we working for farmers?" For Fair Trade to even have a future it must be dynamic, committed to critical questioning, open to new dimensions, and ready for change.

The promise of technology

Consumers can join the debate and help the movement find solutions to the conundrums that are stumping the Fair Trade leadership. We are in the twenty-first century, so let's leave politics and philosophy for the moment and start with technology. Two recent initiatives on the Fair Trade scene are offering the movement new pathways to increase the value craft producers receive. They are also raising questions about the role of Fair Trade intermediaries who distribute and market the products of artisans.

Catalog Generator

Anyone who has purchased a product from a Web site, bid during an eBay auction, or signed up for an online dating service has taken part in e-commerce. As we saw in chapter six, the Internet is providing a new channel for the sale of Fair Trade products. It is also serving as a driving force in connecting fair traders through listservs, electronic mail, blogs, and the like. The Internet is clearly one of the best aspects of globalization.

A recent U.N. Development Programme survey of initiatives in Nepal found that income and employment for small, micro, and medium-size enterprises is dramatically increased thanks to e-commerce. "Firms using [e-commerce] reported sales generated via inquiries to their sites averaging $1,103 per month in 2004 and growing dramatically to $1,852 in July of 2005."

Fair Trade visionary Daniel Salcedo, along with an international team of programmers and producers, has embraced a technological advance known as CatGen, which stands for Catalog Generator. The CatGen platform, which is promoted by Salcedo's non-profit organization, PEOPlink, allows producers to create their own online catalogs that can process orders directly from customers. The CatGen technology requires a laptop, open source software, and a phone line. In an era of cell phones and satellites, these are resources even producers in the remotest locations can access.

In the realm of Fair Trade, such technology allows producers to process orders without working through wholesalers – even Fair Trade importers. And, it allows producers to capture more value along the chain for themselves. Suggesting that the "Fair Trade movement is built on misperceptions ... that the artisan receives most of the value," Salcedo calls into question the role of Fair Trade Organizations that warehouse, export, import, market, and ship products. Salcedo believes these F.T.O.s effectively serve as a "softer face" of the conventional supply chain while retaining the majority of dollar value in Fair Trade transactions. With the availability of technology and shipping services, producers can now control more of their operations. Instead of serving as ethical intermediaries, Salcedo posits the role of "infomediaries" for Fair Trade organizations. Building on the generation-old reputation of Fair Trade credibility and adhering to Fair Trade principles, fair traders can offer transparency in a marketplace crowded with questionable sourcing. F.T.O.s can also help build relationships between producers and consumers by maintaining referral systems that drive particular constituents, such as students or a women's church group, to a "metamarket" of preferred producer partners.

Although retaining more value in countries of origin is clearly a laudable aim, it sometimes bumps up against the realities of implementation. We have seen throughout this guide that Fair Trade producers struggle against the constraints of poverty and isolation. Salcedo tells a great tale of a solar powered cell phone downloading orders on a Brazilian mountaintop. However, by virtue of the fact that some Fair Trade cooperatives and associations have to attend to critical concerns related to the livelihoods of their artisans, they may not have the capacity for real-time negotiated invoicing and other enhancements provided by new technologies and services.

The U.N.D.P. report from Nepal notes that business leaders, such as Bill Gates, Michael Dell, and Steve Jobs, never graduated from college, suggesting that in developing countries "a relatively inexperienced group of young information technology professionals could, with the proper tools, create employment for themselves and [small scale enterprises]." However, the report goes on to suggest that women in particular benefit from e-commerce employment. The overall literacy rate for women in Nepal is only thirty-five percent. While there is clearly potential for utilizing the power of technology in developing countries, the producers of traditional concern to Fair Traders – those who are socially marginalized, for example – may need further development assistance before being able to become e-commerce agents.

Another concern about the use of CatGen is that it is open to any producer group whether or not they meet Fair Trade standards. Salcedo dismisses this concern, saying that groups, such as I.F.A.T., can police the membership of their metamarkets and can remove any groups that aren't in compliance. However, if the role of F.T.O.s is to provide transparent information about the ver-acity of the producer groups, their communication strategies may get muddied as they seek to distinguish between deserving producer groups. As I was navigating around the various sites supported by CatGen, I often had a difficult time distinguishing which group was or was not classified Fair Trade by a third party such as I.F.A.T. Although Salcedo, a long-time development practitioner, is more interested in getting value to producer countries than making distinctions as to who is inside or outside the Fair Trade system, I argue this distinction is crucial for consumers trying to make their way through the crowded marketplace. This is to say that the CatGen technology is an important lightning rod. If the future of Fair Trade is to be relevant, we need to debate and experiment with new approaches to, as Salcedo says, "take advantage of opportunities [within] systems to get as much of the value back to the producer [as possible]."

Wage Guide

Another technology-based tool for artisans was conceived by a new generation of fair traders, the founders of World of Good and its independent non-profit, the World of Good Development Organization (W.O.G.D.O.). The mission of World of Good (W.O.G.), the business, is to make purchasing Fair Trade artisan products easy for the consumer, to help artisans and their communities, and to educate consumers about the benefits of Fair Trade. Ten percent of the company's net profits are reinvested dollar for dollar in the artisan communities in the form of infrastructure and health projects.

Priya Haji and the other founders of W.O.G. share a zealous commitment to helping artisans access the $55 billion American gift market. W.O.G. creates unique shopping opportunities by offering kiosks filled with appealing Fair Trade items to mainstream retailers, such as Wild Oats food stores. With more than a thousand "stores within a store," consumer exposure to Fair Trade products is growing rapidly. W.O.G.D.O. also aspires to set clear, transparent operational standards that will encourage mainstream retailers to adopt Fair Trade purchasing and sourcing practices, thereby improving the lives of thousands of Fair Trade artisans around the world.

A tool for such standard setting is the Fair Trade Wage Guide, provided on a straightforward, user-friendly Web site that helps artisans and traders calculate fair wages. As pointed out in chapter three, the tremendous number of variables involved in handcraft production – including materials used, time spent, and producer location – has made identifying a standard price for crafts difficult. The Fair Trade Wage Guide addresses one element of this dilemma by creating a methodology for calculating fair wages. By providing standardized information, the guide helps ensure that artisans are fairly compensated and also "creates an auditable trail of the transaction for a Fair Trade craft purchase ... and [reinforces] the movement to create a Fair Trade craft product label."

I visited the Wage Guide Web site to test out the hypothetical situation of paying an artisan in Madagascar for the labor involved in making handmade Fair Trade greeting cards. In four straightforward steps, I filled in variables related to the materials and techniques used to create a product. I ended up on a page that evaluated whether or not I had paid a living wage relative to Madagascar's national standards for a minimum wage and the international poverty line. In this case, my projections were well below a living wage. The guide gave me suggestions for making increases. The suggestions were based on the results of a test conducted in cooperation with Mercado Global in Guatemala. As the Web site explains:

Representatives and artisans realized how long it was taking to complete the intricate knotting design work [of a test product] ... [T]he artisans and representatives determined that by cutting the knotting from five inches to three inches in length, they were able to lessen labor time without decreasing the value of the product ... Therefore, the artisans were able to make more of the product in less time, increasing their wage per piece.

This type of advice alongside verifiable wage standards empowers artisans to negotiate with both Fair Trade and conventional traders.

If any wholesaler – Fair Trade or not – is able to use the guide, then the lines between Fair Trade and conventional traders may be blurred. As with the CatGen situation, important distinctions can be lost if consumers think they are supporting Fair Trade enterprises but instead are giving their business to mainstream companies with limited commitments to Fair Trade. Then again, increasing market access is a major priority for artisans. Much like the concerns of mainstreaming labeled food products discussed in chapter three, the Wage Guide calculator opens up debate in the artisan sector as to how to distinguish between mission-based, 100 percent Fair Trade organizations and commercial companies.

The Wage Guide could also create situations where traders will only pay a minimum price because the calculation created holds up the floor price as acceptable. Here, too, this is not a critique limited to artisan products. As Equal Exchange co-founder and current chief executive officer of the Oké U.S.A. Fair Trade fruit company, Jonathan Rosenthal points out, "There is a huge inequality still [in the Fair Trade system] ... to pay producers $1.26 or even $1.50 for a pound of coffee that is selling for $10, nothing is fair about that. Eighty percent of the value is not going to the producer and the labor certainly is eighty percent of the product." Artisans could find that traders will not negotiate beyond the minimum daily wage, although such a minimum may not, given varying circumstances, provide for a sustainable livelihood.

This potential pitfall invites a new opportunity for dialogue and partnership among fair traders, as well as continued analysis into the nature of current trading mechanisms. If equipped with shared information and mutual understanding, artisans and traders could come together around the Wage Guide, and it could develop into another step in the right direction toward poverty reduction and empowerment. As W.O.G.D.O. tests the tool with artisans and traders on several continents, it has gathered an advisory committee to help inform the process and the final result. One participant in the process, Yannina Meza from Peru, has declared that "the Fair Trade Calculator is a dream come true!" With engaged advisors and responsive consumers, the dream may very well be realized.

Although increasing income opportunities and promoting transparency are, as we have seen throughout the guide, cherished aspects of Fair Trade, the Wage Guide and CatGen have encountered some resistance. The roles of traditional Fair Trade Organizations may diminish if artisans are able to set their own prices based on data provided by the Wage Guide. Fair Trade Organizations, often based in the Global North, have a long, distinguished history of contributing to the capacity of, taking risks for, and investing in Fair Trade producer partners. Fair Trade champions have traditionally put the concerns of disenfranchised producers at the center of their efforts. As is often true with managing change, accepting new approaches and shifting activities and risks can be uncomfortable.

Multiple meanings of certification

Earlier we considered the role of the F.L.O. product label in the history and current practice of the movement. The implications of the mainstreaming of Fair Trade cannot be overstated and are central to the future development of the movement. Although Yale University senior researcher Michael Conroy calls certification, "market-based voluntary corporate accountability ... with teeth," the emergence of a label for some Fair Trade food products has proven to be a mixed blessing. By virtue of the fact that "a large part of [the] growth [in the Fair Trade market] would not have been possible without a growing number of commercial partners becoming involved through the Fairtrade labeling schemes," Fair Trade is now confronted with tensions that are a product of its success.

We have seen that mainstream companies have adopted some products without embracing Fair Trade as a business model. Purists, who wish to preserve the highest bar possible for the Fair Trade concept, see this as a dilution of the Fair Trade ideal. With a particularly jaundiced eye toward multinational corporations, some fair traders also see the adoption of the label on a few product lines as an attempt to "fair wash" the deeper realities of business operations or, worse, to dominate the fledgling Fair Trade market as they dominate the conventional value chain. For its part, F.I.N.E. identifies that labeling organizations must "find innovative ways to co-operate with multinationals and still continue to maintain a critical perspective wherever and whenever the corporations act to the detriment of people and/or the environment."

No doubt multinational corporations – past and present – have been guilty of horrific practices. Our society is also replete with attempts to capture customers through deceptive marketing. Corporations are filled with individual human beings, so they are filled with opportunities for redemption and change, as well as for deception and exploitation. Consumers have to evaluate current policies and do business with those companies that most closely match their personal values and priorities. Organizations such as Net-Impact and the Business Ethics Network seek to help ethically minded entrepreneurs influence the corporate world.

Within Fair Trade's own quarters, there are also concerns that the national certifying bodies of F.L.O., when awarding a license to use the Fair Trade labels, are not setting their standards high enough. National initiatives have been accused of being satisfied with adherence to the fair price aspect of fair trading without strictly applying the other principles. Because some corporations, when pushed on issues such as the quantity of their annual Fair Trade purchases, cite confidentiality and propriety information as a reason for not revealing actual commitments to Fair Trade, the principle of transparency is also called into question. Although certifiers, such as TransFair USA, are responding to some specific questions related to the certification system and farmer empowerment, what the label actually means to the company licensing its use and the consumer using it to make meaningful purchasing choices is of particular concern. Brian Backe, who leads the Domestic Programs Support Unit of Catholic Relief Services after more than a decade with SERRV International, laments:

> When people talk about fairness their minds go to money and economic exchange, but in my estimation the money is not the most

important. The relationships, the commitment to advance payments, to being there where your partners are, is every bit as important if not more than the price paid ... The [use of] labeling is a simplified and one dimensional understanding of the trading relationship [offered by Fair Trade].

Concerns about the label are not limited to licensee use. The coffee registry that producers join to enter the Fair Trade system has been plagued with backlogs and, some say, shuts out new producer groups. During a chat at a Fair Trade convergence in early 2006, an executive from Starbucks pointed out to me that Fair Trade is very concerned with promoting long-term relationships. However, if Starbucks were to shift all its purchases to Fair Trade suppliers, it would have to sever ties with family farmers who cannot enter the system by virtue of the fact that they don't meet the requirement of being members of a cooperative. She went on to say that even within the certified system, it is difficult to establish verifiable paper trails when coffee cooperatives exist on two tiers.

The COSURCA cooperative introduced in chapter seven, for example, consists of thirteen first tier cooperatives – groups of farmers who are organized geographically. COSURCA itself is a tier-two cooperative that provides services to approximately 1,700 tier-one farmers. Creating adequate paper trails while working through the tiers is a challenge, particularly in developing countries. F.L.O. has taken steps to address problems with the system, establishing an independent certification structure. "The main reason for the foundation of FLO-Cert as a limited company is to make Fairtrade's certification and trade auditing operations more transparent." Aside from the audit worthiness of the value chain, when farmer associations number in the tens of thousands it calls into question the notion of direct relationships between producers and consumers. More to the point, however, is the perception that the registry is a closed system that only accrues benefits to a limited number of needy farmers. The system is also effectively closed to artisans because there is currently no system to label products, although the pros and cons of such a label are being considered by I.F.A.T., F.L.O., and others in the movement.

Individual consumers have to determine comfort levels with the use of a label and how it does or does not act as a signal of Fair Trade principles.

In a world jammed with messages and symbols, and in the context of tensions within the labeling system, it can be difficult to know which claims are authentic. Producers also have concerns about the meaning of product labels. In a March 2006 declaration, C.L.A.C. – the Latin American and Caribbean Network of Small Fair Trade Producers – pointed out, "We work *in* the market, not only *for* the market. Our participation in the market is not based on a principle of obtaining the maximum price without considering total quality of life" (emphasis mine). Additionally, the network announced an initiative adopting a new symbol for identifying small producers saying "With this initiative and our symbol we promise to continue fighting for a new model of trade with justice."

Although I have not spoken directly with leaders of C.L.A.C., I suspect the declaration signifies a concern that current label use does not sufficiently address producer priorities. However, I have my own concerns that a new symbol clutters an already crowded field of labels. Nevertheless, the point goes beyond the actual label in question. A representative for I.F.A.T.'s Latin American region says, "We need to generate trust in the Fair Trade movement. Fair Trade is a fashionable term, and is poorly used ... We shouldn't be an exclusive movement, but our movement needs the core Fair Trade values over everything." This, too, indicates a preference for a holistic approach to holding fair traders to a high standard. Such an approach is not simple and not easily implemented. A label, symbol, or mark undoubtedly plays a role. The voices and perspectives of consumers need to be involved in the debate as to what such tools mean.

Neighborhood trade

In the same spirit as the U.S. based domestic Fair Trade we considered in chapter eight, fair traders in the Global South are finding ways to promote Fair Trade in their own backyards. As we heard from Priya Haji of World of Good, the potential market for Fair Trade handcrafts in the United States is vast. However, other untapped markets are present in South-to-South trading, wherein producing countries sell to other developing countries, usually in their own region. Domestic markets are also being created through solidarity trade, which has been defined as efforts toward "producing and sharing enough material wealth among all in order to generate sustainable conditions for self-managed development of each and every member of societies, the peoples and the planet." Solidarity trade's values and practices are drawn from the cultures and traditions of the indigenous people of the Global South. The U.S. family farmer efforts described in chapter eight could also be seen as a form of solidarity trade.

Comercio Justo in Mexico was the first southern initiative to develop its own product certification with the intention of selling to local markets, in this case to the Mexican middle class and tourist markets. Brazilian fair traders have garnered support from their federal government and have created the Brazilian Fair Trade Forum, extending the scope of Fair Trade to internal markets. Several countries, such as Ecuador and Kenya, have their own Fair Trade shops. These developments in South-to-South and solidarity trade are encouraging initiatives. Unfortunately, not all initiatives are successful. Fair Trade shops run by Viva Rio in Brazil closed after just a few years in operation. Their failure may reflect a lack of disposable income in developing countries and also points to the need for more consumer awareness and interest in Fair Trade.

Regional and local trade shifts the power dynamic in the historic North-South relations. In fulfillment of Fair Trade aspirations to

PEOPLE ARE MORE IMPORTANT THAN PRICE

One of the "Seven Sins," as Gandhi put it, was: "Commerce without morality." In this way, a fair price is a moral price. It should, however, be clear that paying this price is only part of the overall package that will transform humanity.

I believe we are all in the same boat. The circumstances might vary. But in the end, what touches one part of humanity sooner or later affects the rest.

Ashenafi Argaw, Export Head of Ethiopia's Sidama
Coffee Farmers Cooperative Union

contribute to producer empowerment, these types of trade hold much economic and political promise for artisans and farmers in the future.

Creating the future

As we reflect on the challenges in the Fair Trade movement it seems evident that a phenomenon does not have to be perfect to be valuable. But for Fair Trade to sustain itself as a vibrant, relevant movement it will need to bring together the various visions, ethos, and interests of traders, North and South, global and local. It will require a tireless spirit of introspection in the face of critiques. It will require the flexibility to embrace new concerns, such as those of working class consumers, without losing sight of core commitments. It will require, therefore, a diverse and engaged consumer base.

Readers of this guide are being invited to consider Fair Trade as a movement worthy of their participation. What, then, is being asked of the consumer as she or he considers Fair Trade?

Consumers are trained to be bargain hunters and to get the best deal. They live in a world where cheap, quick and plentiful are considered cutting edge and savvy. Embracing Fair Trade fully is likely to mean changing old habits and patterns. It may mean viewing the world from different perspectives. To do so, consider some questions from *The Conscious Consumer: Promoting Economic Justice Through Fair Trade*:

Is the ultimate goal of Fair Trade to advance an entirely new economic model, one that permanently shifts the means of production – and therefore profits – to workers?

Is it responsible to persuade affluent societies, where most consume resources at an unsustainable pace, to continue consuming, as long as they're buying fairly traded products?

How can Fair Trade producers best develop domestic markets rather than rely heavily on exports?

How can more domestic Fair Trade products be marketed in developed regions?

And, now, on a more personal level:

In an increasingly disconnected, impersonal world is Fair Trade a way to connect authentically with other people in my community, as well as the broader world?

What relevance does Fair Trade have to people struggling in poverty in so called "developed" countries?

How can my purchasing decisions translate into being an effective citizen and neighbor?

Is it possible to translate Fair Trade shopping into opportunities to promote values-based consumption?

Each of us has to answer these types of questions for ourselves, to decide the right level of engagement with potential trading partners around the world. The final chapter of this guide is designed to help you consider some of the possibilities.

10

Daily life with Fair Trade

Overview: an individual consumer and member of society has many opportunities to participate in the Fair Trade movement. In this chapter,
we'll start with a consideration of the household budget and then look
at some ways for community engagement through Fair Trade.

Let's start this chapter with a personal question. In the context of living
wages and minimum prices, let me ask: do you have a household budget? A
spreadsheet, a checkbook register, or even just a simple sheet of paper that
helps you keep track of how much money you have and where it goes?

There is no way for me to know what a reader's unique financial
situation is, but I am very sure that money is a powerful force in your
life. As Joe Dominguez and Vicki Robin set out in *Your Money or Your
Life*, our relationship to money affects not just how we earn, spend, and
save; it also determines how we use time and how we ascribe value to
other people, as well as possessions. A budget is one way consumers can
build thoughtful habits and set goals that reflect their values.

"Buying Fair Trade is like giving a glass of clean water to a thirsty
person," a cocoa farmer once told me. Literally and figuratively, Fair
Trade quenches thirst. For the producers, water wells can be dug and
sanitation provided. Aspirations to provide a brighter future for children
can be realized. For consumers, Fair Trade quenches our thirst, not only
for the products we need in our daily lives, but also for a sustainable
connection to others. This chapter tries to navigate the journey of a
fair trader, starting at the household level and continuing to workplaces,
schools, and places of worship. We'll even consider the possibility of
running a Fair Trade business.

Shifting your dollars

Turning to this idea of a household budget, the Fair Trade Resource
Network (F.T.R.N.), a consumer awareness organization, encourages

each American household to shift five percent of its budget to purchases from Fair Trade Organizations. F.T.R.N. seeks to improve people's
lives through Fair Trade alternatives by providing information, leadership, and inspiration. Its Web site is an information gateway for consumers and features a bibliography of Fair Trade materials and
information. F.T.R.N. is also the lead organizer of World Fair Trade
Day in the United States, and it mentors the United Students for Fair
Trade, an organization focused on student activism (for more information see below).

As the name implies, F.T.R.N. is a network of individuals and organizations. Although it provides actual resources, such as *The Conscious
Consumer*, a fundamental task is to encourage the building of a network
of human resources – individuals who believe in Fair Trade and want
to make it work for both producers and consumers. In chapter six, readers met one of F.T.R.N.'s members, Stephanie Sheerin, who provides a
great model of Fair Trade advocacy. But, Stephanie didn't just arrive on
the planet a Fair Trader. She, and others like her, had to start somewhere.
F.T.R.N. has designed the Fair Trade Challenge as a way to develop the
Fair Trade marketplace through an increase in sales and to encourage
incorporation of Fair Trade into our personal habits.

F.T.R.N. reports that the average U.S. household spends nearly
$8,500 annually on food, clothing, and home furnishings. By challeng-
ing ourselves to shift just five percent of that amount – a mere $425 a
year – we could make a significant contribution to the lives of impoverished people. To put that statistic in perspective, consider that the average *income* for South Asians is less than $500 a year.

Granted, no one poor person is going to get an extra $425 because
of an individual's budget commitment. But each entry into the Fair
Trade system *will* have a ripple effect. First, if a consumer chooses to
support 100 percent Fair Trade Organizations, whether as retail operations, online stores, or wholesalers, money will often be directed to
small, family-owned businesses that have fully embraced Fair Trade
principles and who are competing against multi-million dollar enterprises. Others are non-profit organizations dedicated to a social mission
in support of the struggling producers. The Fair Trade Federation provides a list of its members so you can buy directly from them. The
growth of Fair Trade in recent years also demonstrates that mainstream
business are influenced by the popularity of Fair Trade, with companies

such as Green Mountain Coffee Roasters expanding their product lines to include Fair Trade.

Your money will also reach the country where the product was made. Kaarvan Crafts of Pakistan, a member of the Fair Trade Federation, reports that the household income of the women it works with increased by thirty percent thanks to the employment Kaarvan was able to organize among impoverished women. The word *kaarvan* translates to "process of moving together." With the five percent challenge, consumers have the opportunity to commit themselves to moving together with the women of Pakistan and other developing countries.

Here is a simple exercise to help readers get started. The table can help identify the amount of money available to spend when buying from Fair Trade organizations. Look at income for one month, and then subtract important non-Fair Trade items like rent or health insurance premiums. Pay utilities, put some aside for savings or reducing your credit card debt, and identify whatever the essentials are.

Table 4. Fair Trade Challenge Worksheet for the month of _____

INCOME	Dollars/Pounds/Euros
Subtract housing costs	-
Subtract utilities	-
Subtract transport	-
Subtract health care	-
AMOUNT AVAILABLE FOR FAIR TRADE	=

Some remaining big items will be categories where you have the opportunity to buy Fair Trade. Can you commit to shifting five percent of your groceries – coffee, tea, fruit, and rice – to Fair Trade? What about gifts? Can you begin to purchase your loved ones, friends, and associates gifts that are Fair Trade? Imagine going to a baby shower, and among the typical plastic blocks and stuffed animals, your gift of a handmade multi-colored nursery mobile from the Philippines stands out as unique, inviting, and socially responsible.

Table 5. Calculating Your Personal Fair Trade Challenge Goal

			F.T. Challenge amount
Food budget	$/£/€	Multiply by 0.5	
Clothing budget	$/£/€	Multiply by 0.5	
Gift items	$/£/€	Multiply by 0.5	

This exercise indicates how straightforward the Fair Trade Challenge can be. Although this first step toward Fair Trade commitment is very manageable, its impact can be immense. Co-op America, whose mission is to harness economic power to create a socially just and environmentally sustainable society, reports that Americans spend $14 trillion a year on household expenses, after housing and taxes. Imagine the world if Americans alone shifted five percent of those trillions to opportunities for the women of Pakistan, not only to increase their income, but also to allow them to work in dignity and demonstrate their talents and skills!

Pledging your participation

Recognizing that Fair Trade involvement starts from a personal place, such as commitments to shopping responsibly, Co-op America's Fair Trade Alliance also seeks to support consumers who want to weave Fair Trade into their lives. The Alliance is a diverse collection of organizations that sign up for its pledge by promising to:

Buy Fair Trade Certified™ coffee, tea, cocoa/chocolate, and other certified products as available for meetings and gatherings.
Purchase commodities or crafts from members of the Fair Trade Federation.
Educate classmates, co-workers, and community members about Fair Trade.
Promote Fair Trade through community events or other activities, whenever possible.

A stellar example of a Fair Trade Alliance member that has acted on its pledge is the Young's Service Center in Portland, Maine. Auto repair owners Carl and Mary Harriman extend their commitment to providing a living wage for their employees to a commitment to workers worldwide. They purchase Fair Trade food products for their lunchroom and distribute Fair Trade materials, such as Co-op America's "Guide to Fair Trade," to customers. With support from the Alliance, the Harrimans are progressively increasing their commitment to Fair Trade within the community. These small business owners have begun educating their peers about Fair Trade through membership of their local chamber of commerce.

The Alliance supports this business and a diversity of others, such as a yoga studio and an architectural firm, through Fair Trade materials and information, as well as by providing special offers from Fair Trade businesses. Because the Alliance is a program of Co-op America, Alliance members are also linked to projects, such as the "Adopt-A-Supermarket" campaign. This campaign is designed to ensure that more Fair Trade food products appear on supermarket shelves by building local community pressure to encourage supermarkets to carry and promote Fair Trade products.

Acting up on campus

Moving beyond a single household or workplace, there are possibilities to be a fair trader who converts an entire institution to Fair Trade. Students on more than 350 college campuses have done so. Across the United States and increasingly in Canada, in alliance with organizations, such as Oxfam America and TransFair USA, students have convinced college administrators and food service providers to offer Fair Trade coffee in dining halls and bookstores. Even for those no longer in the classroom, the success of campuses affiliated with United Students for Fair Trade (U.S.F.T.) or the newer Canadian Student Fair Trade Network is an important model for community organizing. As a fair trader, you'll also want to keep in touch with the students in the movement because, as U.S.F.T. national coordinator Joe Curnow promises, students involved in Fair Trade activism while in school will be "shaking things up well beyond graduation."

The students and mentors associated with U.S.F.T. are some of the most creative and energized elements of the U.S. Fair Trade movement.

Since U.S.F.T.'s birth in 2002, the loose-knit and consensus-based organization has distinguished itself by its ability to bring students across the United States together around a common vision and set of values. The key, says Curnow, is U.S.F.T.'s belief that Fair Trade is not just about pushing product:

> We are about empowering students to advocate for what they think is important, building organizational capacity for students and helping them to experience their own power through the process of advocating for something that is very valuable and is in solidarity.

There are several ways students of any country can become fair traders. The most popular and successful starting point is to gather with other students to bring Fair Trade coffee to campuses. Successful campaigns converting dining hall coffee to Fair Trade create tremendous volume increases in Fair Trade coffee sold. It is also a unique learning opportunity as students research talking points, create organizing plans, and make their case for Fair Trade before institutional decision makers. To guide students on best practice, U.S.F.T. has an organizing kit with helpful hints and reproducible material. It is based on a successful campaign at Georgetown University. U.S.F.T. also maintains an active listserv.

U.S.F.T. also utilizes an affiliate structure to support and mobilize actions based on tactics and techniques proven time and time again at campuses large and small. "Affiliates can either be individuals seeking to begin an organization, or already-initiated organizations which intend to engage in Fair Trade action or education as part of their activities. Affiliates, as opposed to chapters, are autonomous organizations or individuals with the desire to advocate for Fair Trade products, principles and policies." As of this writing, there are 100 affiliates in the U.S.F.T. structure, which is organized according to regions and develops peer-to-peer information sharing.

Students from any campus – affiliated or not – are welcome at the annual U.S.F.T. convergence, which happens in the United States over the Presidents' Day holiday each year. What kind of event inspires students to give up a three day weekend and devote themselves to Fair Trade? Curnow notes that the content of the workshops is presented using principles of popular education, the hospitality – from meals

Figure 13 Tabling with free Fair Trade samples at university student centers is a popular way to gather petition signatures and share Fair Trade information.

provided to use of paper products – is driven by a green and vegan sensibility, and the ethos is one where students are offered examples of how they can live their values. Producers have a key role in the convergence, so that students and producers can learn through and with each other about what is appropriate for the Fair Trade movement.

This producer-student learning partnership is the impetus behind U.S.F.T.'s annual "trips to origin." Students interested in Fair Trade, can participate in delegations to countries, such as Nicaragua, where they live among farmers, harvest coffee, and dialogue, dialogue, dialogue in order to ground reflective activism in the life experiences of farmers. In 2006, in partnership with Thanksgiving Coffee and Lutheran World Relief, U.S.F.T organized a unique interfaith journey to Kenya, Tanzania, and Uganda featuring time with the Mirembe Kawomera, a coffee cooperative of Jewish, Muslim, and Christian coffee farmers. Almost twenty students spent a month exploring what role faith did or did not play in their activism, indicating once again U.S.F.T.'s commitment to achieving its vision of "a global economy that empowers communities everywhere through human relationships that are just and based on respect and dignity."

Matching faith with fairness

Such faith based trips to countries where Fair Trade is changing lives are, not surprisingly, an opportunity provided by several religious organizations, such as the Presbyterian Church (U.S.A.) and Lutheran World Relief in the States and Trade Aid in New Zealand. These journeys are usually at least a week long and involve meeting and living with producers, participating in their Fair Trade work, conducting activities for mutual learning, and then returning home impassioned to advocate on behalf of new friends.

Marketing projects based in houses of worship are another approach popular with religious groups. Congregations commit to serving Fair Trade coffee after services and often offer Fair Trade chocolate or coffee for sale to individual parishioners. Fair Trade craft sales conducted in partnership with Fair Trade Organizations, such as A Greater Gift or Ten Thousand Villages, are also special events, particularly around the Christmas and Hanukkah seasons when gift giving is a prime time to draw connections between consumption and values.

Not only do these types of sales help disadvantaged producers sell to a sympathetic customer base, but they also provide regular "teachable moments" when parishioners can be educated about how their visions of economic justice can be made manifest in the lives of Fair Trade artisans and farmers. Mutual empowerment takes place as farmers and artisans improve the lives of their families and communities. By buying Fair Trade, parishioners make powerful choices that are in alignment with the imperatives of their faith.

Lutheran World Relief (L.W.R.) took a special role in leveraging interfaith power to promote Fair Trade and trade justice issues. The Interfaith Fair Trade Initiative (I.F.T.I.), coordinated by L.W.R., was a key force in a 2003 decision by Procter & Gamble, the largest seller of coffee in the U.S., to introduce Fair Trade Certified™ coffee products through its specialty coffee division, Millstone. The decision came in response to dialogue with shareholders about the company's practices, as well as pressure from advocacy groups, such as I.F.T.I. Former I.F.T.I. director Sarah Ford explains:

> The Lutheran faith asks that we "act justly and love mercy"; and to that end, L.W.R. was part of a nation-wide coalition of faith, secular, and student organizations asking P&G to sell five percent, or 2.5 million tons, of their coffee as Fair Trade over three years. They prevented a potential negative association millions of people of faith would have to the P&G brands by taking this step in the direction of economic justice.

David Avrill, a member of the Catholic Relief Services (C.R.S.) Fair Trade Network, once explained to me his parish based involvement in Fair Trade: "It is one thing to pray and become aware of injustices. But it is also another thing to try and find ways to act … I wanted to be a part of systematic change. I didn't want to be sentimental in my faith."

Taking it to your town

In a nice intersection of faith and secular concerns, Fairtrade Towns in the United Kingdom is encouraging places of worship, businesses, schools, and government agencies to claim the title "Fairtrade Town." Bruce Crowther, Fairtrade Towns' coordinator, reports that as of early 2006 there were 186 Fairtrade Towns in the United Kingdom with Oslo, Norway, expecting recognition by the end of 2006. In yet another example of how individual consumers can have a significant role to play in the Fair Trade movement, concerned volunteers, who wanted to spread the message and build the marketplace for Fair Trade, started the town concept. In the small town of Garstang in northwest England, Crowther and other members of the local Oxfam group decided to invite local leaders to a meal in support of Fair Trade. The group invited government officials and business representatives to the meal, consisting of both locally grown and fairly traded products. The meal was part of an annual celebration of Fair Trade called "Fairtrade Fortnight" that occurs every March. It inspired residents to vote to make Garstang the first Fairtrade Town at a public meeting in April 2000. The designation quickly spread through the United Kingdom, thanks in part to recognition by the Under Secretary of State for the Department of International Development, who congratulated Garstang by saying, "The beacon that has started in Garstang can spread like wildfire through the whole country."

In the United Kingdom, the Fairtrade Foundation, the national initiative of Fairtrade Labeling Organizations International (see chapter three), coordinates the application process for town designation. The goals that are evaluated are:

Local council passes a resolution supporting Fairtrade★ and agrees to serve Fairtrade★ tea and coffee at its meetings and in its offices and canteens.

A range of (at least two) Fairtrade★ products are readily available in the area's shops and local cafés/catering establishments.

Fairtrade★ products are used by an appropriate number of local work places (estate agents, hairdressers, etc., for a small town, and a large flagship employer for a large town or city) and community organizations (churches, schools, universities, etc.).

Attract media coverage and popular support for the campaign.

A local Steering Group is convened to ensure progress and continued commitment to the campaign.

Using this initiative as its model, communities in the United States are pursuing the Fair Trade town concept. Supported by Oxfam America and TransFair USA, Fair Trade coalitions have begun exploring the concept in Boston, Chicago, Los Angeles, New York, San Diego, San Francisco, and Seattle.

Kimberly Easson, vice president of strategic relations for TransFair USA, encapsulates why Fairtrade Towns are so appealing:

Fairtrade Towns foster a level of relationship and collaboration that can help get a message out in a meaningful way. If it is your neighbor that is talking about Fair Trade versus some publication or advertisement you are going to receive that communication differently and perhaps be more open.

If you think your neighbors could be educated and transformed by Fair Trade, learn from the work of past coalitions and organize efforts

★ In the United Kingdom, the Fairtrade Labelling Organization national initiative spells "Fair Trade" as one word. The products refer to those certified by the Fairtrade Foundation.

that make sense for your locale. TransFair USA maintains a list of coalitions pursuing grassroots activism in the United States, as do TransFair Canada and the U.K.'s Fairtrade Foundation.

Building fairer businesses

Despite the Fair Trade movement's significant growth in recent years, there is a major barrier to continued success, particularly in North America: Fair Trade businesses are far-flung and access to fairly traded organizations and products is not always convenient. If there were more Fair Trade shops and more online commerce, consumers could more readily take the Fair Trade challenge, pledge more advocacy, and act locally on their values.

The Internet is particularly helpful for getting at this dilemma, and a Canadian business called Peri Dar has shown that one entrepreneur with a mission can create a unique shopping experience for the Web-savvy. Nicole McGrath heard on a Radio Canada segment that no Fair Trade businesses existed in Canada – apparently the journalist overlooked Ten Thousand Villages Canada and La Siembra Cooperative – and McGrath determined that she could start one herself. McGrath explained:

> It was important to start a project whose model would appeal to other solo entrepreneurs. Many would-be entrepreneurs today want their future business to be an ethical one and visibly so. Fair Trade is growing rapidly as a movement and [is] the new differentiator. The commitment to Fair Trade wins the business credibility and trust.

Much like the women artisans she seeks to partner with, McGrath opened a home-based business. She launched a bilingual Web site and now offers hundreds of items from bed and bath accessories to children's toys through Peri Dar.

No matter how appealing and helpful the Internet can be, the need for retail locations can never be eliminated. Shoppers like to touch the objects they are considering and, in the case of clothing, trying on options is sometimes helpful. Not to mention the times when a shopper needs to purchase a last-minute gift or replenish a pantry's stock of coffee or tea.

Operating a Fair Trade shop is a way to help meet growing consumer demand for Fair Trade products, create more business for Fair Trade producers, and infuse a community with Fair Trade activity. It is also a way to embody Fair Trade practices as a career path, even for those without a business background.

In 1996, anthropologist Kimberly Grimes and musician Marco Hernandez decided to use their appreciation for other cultures and their desire to create a better world to start Made by Hand International Cooperative. Located in a shopping complex near Bethany Beach, Delaware, just a short bike ride from the couple's solar powered home, the store transports its customers to different continents with lovely tapestries on the walls and world music playing in the background. Never missing an opportunity to educate, Hernandez and Grimes also set up an information rack about Fair Trade and decorated the dressing rooms with Fair Trade facts.

This sharing of the Fair Trade message through educational materials, as well as wonderful product lines, is at the heart of the Made by Hand mission. In her book, *A Guide for Retailers: Creating a Successful Fair Trade Business*, Grimes asserts Fair Trade retailers are on the front line of consumer education:

> We're the face of Fair Trade for ordinary citizens ... Engaging in that daily, face-to-face interaction with people is how we spread the Fair Trade message. As retailers, we must be vibrant and willing to reach out into the community to teach, to listen, to share, to inspire.

I visited Made by Hand for the store's celebration of World Fair Trade Day 2006, joining the crowd sampling Fair Trade salsa and enjoying mini concerts by Hernandez and his band, Katari. Children played with Fair Trade toys while grown-ups eyed everything from patio candles to sweat-free clothing. I noticed customers taking the time to read the producer stories strategically placed on shelves. Hernandez and Grimes make an effort to circulate products and producer profiles to high traffic areas in the store. In this way, they ensure that a range of producers and their handwork receive equal opportunities to catch the customer's eye.

They also work to make sure other potential entrepreneurs understand the ins and outs of being Fair Trade business owners. They mentor potential and current shop owners, hoping to encourage others to join the Fair Trade ranks. This Made by Hand mission is focused on both increasing the number of producers supported and on changing the way business is conducted. With only about 300 stores exclusively devoted to selling Fair Trade in the entire United States and a mere 20 or so in countries such as Australia, opportunities for creating new retail opportunities abound. Even if you live in the United Kingdom, which has an abundance of shops, you can become involved in their work by contacting groups such as the British Association of Fair Trade Shops.

Conclusion: what's at stake?

I once heard a group of Fair Trade activists announce: "This is a movement, let's move!" Which direction Fair Trade should move in, though, is a bit unclear. The Fair Trade movement is replete with examples of how Fair Trade works and why; yet, with more than six decades of history, Fair Trade is at a crossroads.

The inherent appeal of Fair Trade, the comprehensiveness of the model, and the rightness of Fair Trade's concerns have attracted a multitude of participants with an equal number of interpretations of what Fair Trade means. Is Fair Trade a way of reforming or revolutionizing capitalism? Should it work to stay unique and alternative, or should it move toward the mainstream and increased popularity? Is Fair Trade a North-South dynamic or should it – could it – apply to domestic and national economies? Does it help enough of the most disadvantaged producers in the most deprived areas, or is it limited to a certain type of farmer or particular regions? Can trade be fair? Can we sustain a market of equitable exchange? The questions are there for the asking. Each effort to find an answer, to suggest a solution, is a step in the right direction.

If we don't strive to create trading relationships based on fairness, we ignore the freedom of choice our economies offer us. We relinquish the power of combined action to address common, age-old problems. We forfeit opportunities to create widespread solutions based on dialogue, transparency, and respect.

A market is a gathering of people engaged in buying and selling. A market is the time for such a gathering. A market is the people who have gathered.

The Latin word *mercatus* translates as both market and fair.

What does it take to make a pound of coffee? You need thousands of coffee beans, Fair Trade or not. One bean alone is not enough. Many beans must come together to make a cup of coffee. The beans and our actions: they add up. By coming together, beans are transformed – translated, if you will – into coffee. Our particular gatherings known as markets contain the same potential for transformation. In our time together, let us bring the fair back to the market.

References

Chapter One

2 **Fair Trade Definition**   Krier, J.M. (2005). *Fair Trade in Europe 2005: Facts and Figures on Fair Trade in 25 European Countries*. Fair Trade Advocacy Office: Brussels, p. 21.

3 **the four billion impoverished people**   Prahalad, C.K. and Hart, S.L. (2002). "The fortune at the bottom of the pyramid." *strategy + business*, Issue 26, pp. 3–4.

5 **Success will require sustained action**   United Nations (2002). *The United Nations Role Implementing the Millennium Development Goals*. United Nations Department of Public Information: New York, p. 2.

7 **the neutral, invisible market**   Tiffen, P. (2005). "The troubling nature of free trade." Keynote address. *Fair Trade Futures*. Chicago. 1 October.

7 **the best things in life**   De Graff, J., Wann, D., and Naylor, T. (2002). *Affluenza: The All-Consuming Epidemic*. Berrett-Koehler Publishers: San Francisco, p. 8.

7 **first time the term "Fair Trade" was used**   Wills, C. (2006). "Fair trade: what's it all about?" *Business Unusual: Successes and Challenges of Fair Trade*. Fair Trade Media: Newcastle-upon-Tyne, UK.

Chapter Two

10 **A value chain describes**   Tiffen, P., MacDonald, J., Maamah, H., and Osei-Opare, F. (2004). "From tree-minders to global players: Cocoa Farmers in Ghana." *Chains of Fortune: Linking Women Producers and Workers with Global Markets*. Commonwealth Secretariat: London, p. 202.

12 **Influential book**   Brown, M.B. (1993). *Fair Trade: Reform and Realities in the International Trading System*. Zed Books: London, p. 70.

12 **traditional analysis of supply chains** Raynolds, L. (2002). "Consumer/producer links in fair trade coffee networks." *Sociologia Rualis*, Volume 42, pp. 405–424.

13 **Classic liberal economist** Wolf, M. (2004). *Why Globalization Works*. Yale University Press: New Haven, p. 157.

13 **He goes on to say** Wolf, M. (2004). *Why Globalization Works*. Yale University Press: New Haven, p. 172.

14 **May 2006 report** The National Labor Committee. "The National Labor Committee: Putting a Human Face on the Global Economy," available at http://www.nlcnet.org.

15 **as Pauline Tiffen has pointed out** Tiffen, P. (2005). "The troubling nature of free trade." Conference presentation. *Fair Trade Futures*. Chicago. 1 October.

15 **priorities of Fair Traders** Wills, C. (2006). "Fair trade: what's it all about?' *Business Unusual: Successes and Challenges of Fair Trade*. Fair Trade Media: Newcastle-upon-Tyne, UK.

17 **obstacles producers confront** Nicholls, A. and Opal, C. (2005). *Fair Trade: Market-Driven Ethical Consumption*. Sage Publications: London, pp. 33–40.

17 **Naomi Klein critically reveals** Klein, N. (2002). *No Logo: No Space, No Choice, No Jobs*. Picador: New York.

19 **Center for a New American Dream** Tilford, D. (2006). Interview with Jacqueline DeCarlo, April.

19 **Fair Trade shop co-owner** Grimes, K. and Hernandez, M. (2006). Interview with Jacqueline DeCarlo, 13 May.

Chapter Three

21 **products made in China or Taiwan** Letelier, W.L. (2005). Personal communication, 8 August.

21 **"mindless, sexless Barbie doll"** Letelier, W.L. (2005). Personal communication, 8 August.

23 **"In an unprecedented international joint venture"** Tiffen, P. (2002). "A chocolate-coated case for alternative international business models." *Development in Practice*, Volume 12, p. 8.

23 **British Government Millennium Award** Tiffen, P. (2002). "A chocolate-coated case for alternative international business models." *Development in Practice*, Volume 12, p. 8.

24 **also as owners** Meier, B. (2006). Interview with Jacqueline DeCarlo, January.

25 **Fair Trade as "enormous"** Ohemeng-Tinyase, K. (2005). "On Fair Trade benefits to Kuapa Kokoo farmers in Ghana." Keynote address. *Fair Trade Futures.* Chicago. 30 September.

26 **The country of Ghana** Catholic Relief Services. "CRS Fair Trade," available at http://www.crsfairtrade.org.

26 **coming off the shelf** Morton, B. (2005). Interview with Jacqueline DeCarlo, November.

26 **some educational material?** Morton, B. (2005). Interview with Jacqueline DeCarlo, November.

27 **back for next week** Morton, B. (2005). Interview with Jacqueline DeCarlo, November.

29 **World Fair Trade Week in May** Fair Trade Toronto. "Fair Trade Toronto," available at http://www.fairtradetoronto.com.

30 **the foreign and exotic** Littrell, M. and Dickson, M. (1999). *Social Responsibility in the Global Market: Fair Trade of Cultural Products.* Sage Publications: Thousand Oaks, CA, p. 52.

30 **"green or ethical"** Nicholls, A. and Opal, C. (2005). *Fair Trade: Market-Driven Ethical Consumption.* Sage Publications: London, p. 182.

30 **civil rights and anti-war** Zinn, H. (1995). *People's History of the United States: 1492-Present.* HarperCollins: New York, p. 562.

30 **the energy crisis of 1977** Carter, J. (1982). *Keeping Faith: Memoirs of a President.* Bantam Books: Toronto, New York, p. 92.

30 **a record figure of $4 billion** Krier, J.-M. (2008). *Fair Trade 2007: New Facts and Figures from an Ongoing Success Story: A Report on Fair Trade in 33 Consumer Countries.* Fair Trade Advocacy Office: Brussels.

30 **$31 billion in 2003** Nicholls, A. and Opal, C. (2005). *Fair Trade: Market-Driven Ethical Consumption.* Sage Publications: London, p. 182.

30 **health concerns of consumers** Bacon, C. (2005). "Confronting the coffee crisis: can Fair Trade, organic and specialty coffees reduce small-scale farmer vulnerability in northern Nicaragua?" *World Development,* Volume 33, p. 500.

31 **their livelihood: their land** Pomeroy, T. (2006). Interview with Jacqueline DeCarlo, May.

31 **environmentally sustainable Fair Trade fruit** Fairtrade Foundation. "Fairtrade," available at http://www.fairtrade.org.uk.

32 **raw materials for future wood carvings** Musch, C. (2005). Personal communication, November.

32 **250 million children** International Labor Rights Fund. "International Labor Rights Fund," available at http://www.laborrights.org.

33 **working fifteen–hour days** Mobert, D. (1999). "Bringing down Niketown," *The Nation*, 7 June, p. 15.

33 **widespread textile strikes** Zinn, H. (1995). *People's History of the United States: 1492-Present*. HarperCollins: New York, p. 388.

33 **bore the Duke logo** Featherstone, L. and Henwood, D. (2001). "Clothes encounters: activists and economists clash over sweatshops," *Lingua Franca*, March, p. 28.

33 **the students and others** Van Der Werf, M. (2000). "Sweatshop issue escalates with sit-ins and policy shifts," *The Chronicle of Higher Education*, 10 March, p. A38.

33 **abusers of factory workers' rights** Claeson, B. (2005). "Locating the opportunities in the anti–sweatshop movement." Conference presentation. *Constructing Markets for Conscientious Apparel Consumers Conference*. Ann Arbor, MI. 1–2 April.

34 **ban on child labor** Trombetta, M. (2001). "Anti–sweatshop law soon in force in San Francisco," *The Daily Review*, online newspaper available at http://www.sweatfree.org, accessed 15 September.

35 **claiming both free trade perks** Nueva Vida. "The Fair Trade Zone: A Women's Sewing Cooperative," available at http://www. fairtradezone.jhc-cdca.org.

35 **sustainable development and poverty eradication** Trade Justice Movement. "Trade Justice Movement," available at http://www.tjm.org.uk.

36 **the population of Sweden** Statistics Sweden. "Statistics Sweden," available at http://www.scb.se.

36 **exploit disadvantaged peoples** Raynolds, L.T. (2000). "Re-embedding agriculture: the international organic and fair trade movements." *Agriculture and Human Values*, Volume 17, p. 298.

37 **a mode of existence** Martel, Y. (2004). "Fair trade deserves our support," *Globe Mail*, 6 May, Op-Ed.

37 **those who are less fortunate** Martel, Y. (2004). "Fair trade deserves our support," *Globe Mail*, 6 May, Op-Ed.

Chapter Four

40 **children and adult members**   Cafédirect. "Cafédirect — Fairtrade Tea, Fairtrade Coffee and Fairtrade Drinking Chocolate," available at http: //www.cafedirect.co.uk.

40 **local and regional levels**   Oxfam International, Junta Nacional del Café and Oromia Coffee Farmers Cooperative Union (2006). "Grounds for change: creating a voice for small coffee farmers and farmworkers with the next international coffee agreement," April newsletter, p. 5.

40 **twenty-five percent in 2009**   TransFair USA (2010). *Almanac: 2009.* Oakland, CA.

43 **The origins of RUGMARK**   Smith, N. (2006). Personal communication, April.

43 **Santiago's participation**   Funkhouser, D. (2006). Interview with Jacqueline DeCarlo, 24 February.

44 **democratically-controlled enterprise**   International Co-operative Alliance. "International Co-operative Alliance," available at http: //www.coop.org.

45 **and democratic control**   Wilhoit, J. (2005). "Cooperatives: a short history." *Cultural Survival Quarterly*, Issue 29.3, 19 September, available at http: //www.cs.org/ publications/csq/csq-article.cfm?id =1848.

45 **cooperatives earned in Africa**   Tiffen, P., MacDonald, J., Maamah, H. and Osei-Opare, F. (2004). "From tree-minders to global players: cocoa farmers in Ghana." *Chains of Fortune: Linking Women Producers and Workers with Global Markets*. Commonwealth Secretariat: London, p. 35.

45 **cultural or gender bias**   International Fair Trade Association. "IFAT Code of Practice," available at http: //www.ifat.org/downloads/monitoringdownloads.shtml.

46 **high levels of water**   African Home. "African Home Creating Crafts Creating Employment," available at http: //www.africanhome.co.za.

46 **not being too dogmatic**   Gorman, E. (2006). Interview with Jacqueline DeCarlo, 16 March.

47 **International Fair Trade Association**   International Fair Trade Association. "IFAT Code of Practice," available at http: //www.ifat.org/downloads/monitoringdownloads.shtml.

47 **involves independent consultants**   Durwael, S. (2005). "Spectrum of fair trade: IFAT's perspective." Conference presentation. *Fair Trade Futures*. Chicago. 1 October.

49 **If you come to shop**   Dirks, D. (2006). Interview with Jacqueline DeCarlo, 21 October.

51 **800,000 families**   Fairtrade Labeling Organizations International. "FLO International', available at http: //www.fairtrade.net.

51 **100 million pounds of Fair Trade Certified™ coffee**   Funkhouser, D. (2006). Interview with Jacqueline DeCarlo, 24 February.

51 **I think increasingly**   Chase, B. (2006). Interview with Jacqueline DeCarlo, 19 February.

54 **many multinationals insist**   Nestlé S.A., Public Affairs (2005). *The Nestlé Commitment to Africa*. March Report. Vevy, Switzerland.

54 **Taking the high road**   Harris, B. (2006). Interview with Jacqueline DeCarlo, May.

55 **the radical, transformative message of Fair Trade**   Low, W. and Davenport, E. (2005). "Has the medium (roast) become the message?" *International Marketing Review*, Volume 22, pp. 494–511.

55 **We are seeing applicants**   Geffner, D. (2006). Interview with Jacqueline DeCarlo, April.

55 **Partial commitment to Fair Trade**   Low, W. and Davenport, E. (2005). "Has the medium (roast) become the message?" *International Marketing Review,* Volume 22, pp. 494–511.

56 **Starbucks is the largest purchaser**   Starbucks (2006). "Starbucks, fair trade, and coffee social responsibility." Fact Sheet. 7 March.

Chapter Five

57 **she expanded the number of products**   Hess, I. (1995). "SELF HELP Crafts of the world: the first 50 years." Draft of thesis submitted for M.F.A., p. 8.

57 **Byler contributed more than $500**   Hess, I. (1995). "SELF HELP Crafts of the world: the first 50 years." Draft of thesis submitted for M.F.A., p. 8.

58 **the "Needlework Lady"**   Ten Thousand Villages (2004). *Ten Thousand Villages: Cultivating Hundreds of Cultures*. Ten Thousand Villages: Akron, PA.

58 **hired as a part-time manager** Hess, I. (1995). "SELF HELP Crafts of the world: the first 50 years." Draft of thesis submitted for M.F.A., p. 9.

59 **India is not to be found in its few cities** Ten Thousand Villages (2004). *Ten Thousand Villages: Cultivating Hundreds of Cultures.* Ten Thousand Villages: Akron, PA.

59 **It also works with volunteers** Ten Thousand Villages (2004). *Ten Thousand Villages: Cultivating Hundreds of Cultures.* Ten Thousand Villages: Akron, PA.

59 **Right from the beginning** Dirks, D. (2006). Interview with Jacqueline DeCarlo, 21 October.

59 **ordinary people in small places** Myers, P. (2006). Interview with Jacqueline DeCarlo, 21 October.

60 **We use resources carefully** Ten Thousand Villages (2004). *Ten Thousand Villages: Cultivating Hundreds of Cultures.* Ten Thousand Villages: Akron, PA.

60 **We have to be conscious about dependency** Myers, P. (2006). Interview with Jacqueline DeCarlo, 21 October.

61 **baskets, placemats, hand-carved stool**s Ten Thousand Villages. "Ten Thousand Villages," available at http: //www. tenthousandvillages.com/catalog/artisan.detail.php?artisan_id=29 .

61 **many women in Uganda** Ten Thousand Villages. "Ten Thousand Villages," available at http: //www. tenthousandvillages.com/catalog/artisan.detail.php?artisan_id=29 .

62 **is a connection to the community** Dirks, D. (2006). Interview with Jacqueline DeCarlo, 21 October.

62 **goals of SERRV founders** Chase, B. (2006). Interview with Jacqueline DeCarlo, 19 February.

63 **SERRV became an independent nonprofit organization** SERRV (1981). *The SERRV Story: International Handcrafts for SELF HELP.* SERRV: New Windsor, MD.

63 **grow beyond SERRV** Musch, C. (2006). Personal communication, 5 April.

63 **looking at the plants around me** Musch, C. (2006). Interview with Jacqueline DeCarlo, 2 February.

64 **Illiterate or semi-literate men and women** Wills, C. (2006). "Handicrafts: valuing creativity." *Business Unusual: Successes and Challenges of Fair Trade.* Fair Trade Media: Newcastle-upon-Tyne, UK.

64 **humanitarian organizations, such as Oxfam** Nicholls, A. and Opal, C. (2005). *Fair Trade: Market-Driven Ethical Consumption*. Sage Publications: London, p. 21.

64 **Fair trade became part of the strategy** Low, W. and Davenport, E. (2005). "Postcards from the edge: maintaining the alternative character of fair trade." *Sustainable Development*, Volume 13, pp. 143–153.

64 **The first such World Shop** Kocken, M. (2004). "Fifty years of fair trade." International Fair Trade Association: London. January.

65 **Dutch advocates boycotted Angolan coffee** Durwael, S. (2005). "A (short) history of fair trade." Conference presentation. *Fair Trade Futures*. Chicago. 1 October.

65 **Guatemalan coffee from Fair Trade sources** Kocken, M. (2004). "Fifty years of fair trade." International Fair Trade Association: London. January, p. 4.

66 **Members of the Northeast Cooperative**s Rosenthal, J. (2005). "The U.S. fair trade coffee movement: a brief history." *Reaching for another level: strengthening the fair trade coffee movement in the U.S.A.* Draft manuscript. February.

66 **Members of the Northeast Cooperatives** Ericson, R.B. (2006). *The Conscious Consumer: Promoting Economic Justice through Fair Trade.* Fair Trade Resource Network: Washington, DC, p. 14.

66 **average annual sales growth of twenty-four percent** Equal Exchange (2004). *Annual Report*, available at http://www.equalexchange.com/2004-annual-report, p. 11.

66 **coffee, tea, sugar, cocoa, and chocolate bars** Equal Exchange (2004). *Annual Report,* available at http://www.equalexchange.com/2004-annual-report, p. 10.

66 **they custom built Equal Exchang**e North, R. (2003). "Building mission into structure at Equal Exchange," *Business Ethics Magazine*, Volume 17, Summer 2003.

66 **organize themselves democratically** Equal Exchange (2004). *Annual Report*, available at http://www.equalexchange.com/2004-annual-report, p. 11.

66 **another innovation** Equal Exchange. "Equal Exchange: About Our Co-Op," available at http://www.equalexchange.com/story.

67 **immense economic needs** Berman, V. (2006). Personal communication, 19 May.

67 **facilitate exportation to the North**   Kocken, M. (2004). "Fifty years of fair trade." International Fair Trade Association: London. January, p. 2.

67 **artisan employment and empowerment**   Littrell, M. and Dickson, M. (1999). *Social Responsibility in the Global Market: Fair Trade of Cultural Products*. Sage Publications: Thousand Oaks, CA, p. 164.

68 **redesign the destinies of their children**   Marketplace (2006). *Spring/Summer Catalog*.

68 **almost exclusively apparel**   Freitas, P. (2006). Interview with Jacqueline DeCarlo, 12 February.

69 **Where do I stand?**   Freitas, P. (2006). Interview with Jacqueline DeCarlo, 12 February.

69 **Economic development is only the first step**   Freitas, P. (2006). Interview with Jacqueline DeCarlo, 12 February.

69 **sell directly to coffee buyers in industrialized countries**   Green, G. and Warning, M. (2006). "Microeconomic considerations about Fair Trade coffee. The impact of migration on coffee production in Southern Mexico." Proposed conference presentation. *XXVI International Congress of the Latin American Studies Association*. San Juan, Puerto Rico.

70 **We don't want charity**   Buyer Be Fair (2006). "Buyer Be Fair: The Promise of Product Certification." Video transcript, available at http://www.buyerbefair.org, p. 6.

70 **a fictional character in Dutch literature**   Nicholls, A. and Opal, C. (2005). *Fair Trade: Market-Driven Ethical Consumption*. Sage Publications: London, p. 127.

70 **an independent system to verify claims**   Young, G. (2003). "Fair trade's influential past and the challenges of its future." King Baudouin Foundation. May, pp. 5–6.

70 **At much the same time**   Wiehoff, D. (2006). Interview with Jacqueline DeCarlo, 26 September.

70 **its own Fair Trade coffee brand**   Peace Coffee. "Peace Coffee," available at http://www.peacecoffee. com/history.htm.

70 **consultation with groups**   Wiehoff, D. (2006). Interview with Jacqueline DeCarlo, 26 September.

70 **By 1998**   Transfair USA. "Transfair USA," available at http://www.transfairusa. org/content/about/aboutus.php.

70 **certifier to the north** Transfair Canada. "Transfair Canada," available at http://www.transfair.ca.

70 **more than 150 million** Funkhouser, D. (2006). Interview with Jacqueline DeCarlo, 13 October.

Chapter Six

73 **a record figure of $4 billion** Krier, J.-M. (2008). *Fair Trade 2007: New Facts and Figures from an Ongoing Success Story: A Report on Fair Trade in 33 Consumer Countries.* Fair Trade Advocacy Office: Brussels.

73 **$200 million for more than 219 farmer groups** TransFair USA (2009). *Almanac: 2009.* Oakland, CA.

73 **seventy percent of households were regularly buying** Fairtrade Foundation. "Annual Review 2008/2009: Raising awareness and sales," available at Web site: http://www.fairtrade.org.uk/annual_review/awareness_and_sales/.

73 **40,000 retail outlets** Transfair USA (2005). 2005 Fair Trade Coffee Facts and Figures, available at http://transfairusa.org/content/Downloads/ 2005Q2FactsandFigures. pdf.

73 **100,000 Europeans** Krier, J.-M. (2005). *Fair Trade in Europe 2005: Facts and Figures on Fair Trade in 25 European Countries.* Fair Trade Advocacy Office: Brussels, p. 7.

73 **North America and the Pacific Rim in 2003** Fair Trade Federation (2005). *Fair Trade Trends in North America and the Pacific Rim,* available at http://www.equiterre.org/equitable/pdf/ 2005_FTF_Trends_Report.pdf, p. 6.

74 **forty-six percent of the value of Fair Trade products** Fair Trade Federation (2005). *Fair Trade Trends in North America and the Pacific Rim,* available at http://www.equiterre.org/equitable/pdf/ 2005_FTF_Trends_Report.pdf, p. 6.

74 **lives of the "untouchables"** SERRV. "SERRV," available at http://www.agreatergift.org/ ArtisansFarmers/Asia/India.aspx.

74 **Producers working with Tara** Tara Projects. "Tara Projects," available at http://www.taraprojects.com/ aboutus.htm.

75 **"has become a leading voice in the movement"** SERRV. "SERRV," available at http://www.agreatergift.org/ ArtisansFarmers/Asia/India.aspx.

76 **a desk at a software company** Sheridan, M. (2006). Interview with Jacqueline DeCarlo, 9 May.

76 **"limited, exploitative, and often dangerous employment possibilities"** MacHenry, R. (2002). "Building on local strengths: Nepalese fair trade textiles' in *Artisans and Cooperatives: Developing Alternative Trade for the Global Economy*, K. M. Grimes and B. L. Milgram, eds. The University of Arizona Press: Tucson, AZ, p. 27.

76 **a set of indicators** MacDonald, J. (2000). "Measuring the impact of fair trade." *Crafts News*, Volume 11, Issue 44, p. 4.

76 **required for a means of living** Department for International Development (1999). *Sustainable Livelihoods Guidance Sheets*. April, p. 1.

77 **these constraints and opportunities** Department for International Development (1999). *Sustainable Livelihoods Guidance Sheets*. April, p. 5.

77 **Her holistic analysis** Mukheerjee, N. (2005). "Broad-Basing Fair Trade in India: a case study of women, artisan and weaver groups from West Bengal—a holistic approach towards capacity enhancement, sustainable livelihoods and MDGs." Conference presentation. *Fair Trade Futures*. Chicago. 2 October.

78 **few extra cents for the beans** Alsever, J. (2006). "Fair prices for farmers: simple ideas, complex reality," *The New York Times*, 19 March, available at http: //www. nytimes. com/2006/03/19/business/yourmoney/19fair.html?ex=1300424400&en=52f0cde02ecff559&ei=5088&partner=rssnyt&emc=rss.

78 **in the mountains of Mexico** Alsever, J. (2006). "Fair prices for farmers: simple ideas, complex reality," *The New York Times*, 19 March, available at http: //www.nytimes. com/2006/03/19/business/yourmoney/19fair.html?ex=1300424400&en=52f0cde02ecff559&ei=5088&partner=rssnyt&emc=rss.

79 **future discussions about coffee pricing**s Firl, M. "Fair Trade," available at http: //www.alternativegrounds.com.

79 **the needs of the producers** Nash, J. (2002). "To market, to market. Artisans and Cooperatives: Developing Alternative Trade for the Global Economy" in *Artisans and Cooperatives: Developing Alternative Trade for the Global Economy*, K. M. Grimes and B. L. Milgram, eds. The University of Arizona Press: Tucson, AZ, p. 159.

80 **For example, Kuapa Kokoo** Tiffen, P., MacDonald, J., Maamah, H. and Osei-Opare, F. (2004). "From tree-minders to global players:

cocoa farmers in Ghana." *Chains of Fortune: Linking Women Producers and Workers with Global Markets.* Commonwealth Secretariat: London, p. 13.

80 **The Fair Trade certification system emerged**   Green, G. and Warning, M. (2006). "Microeconomic considerations about Fair Trade coffee. The impact of migration on coffee production in Southern Mexico." Conference presentation. *XXVI International Congress of the Latin American Studies Association.* San Juan, Puerto Rico.

80–81 **As development practitioners**   Sheridan, M. (2006). Interview with Jacqueline DeCarlo, 9 May.

Chapter Seven

83 **Cafédirect was intentionally created**   Redfern, A. and Snedker, P. (2002). "Creating market opportunities for small enterprises: experiences of the fair trade movement." SEED Working Paper. International Labour Organization. Report 30, p. 15.

83 **the fourth largest roast and ground coffee brand**   Cafédirect. "Cafédirect," available at http: //www.cafedirect.co.uk/about/index.php.

83 **a partner and friend**   Twin. "Twin," available at http: //www.twin. org.uk/about.html.

83 **a Ghanaian farmer association**   Tiffen, P., MacDonald, J., Maamah, H. and Osei-Opare, F. (2004). "From tree-minders to global players: cocoa farmers in Ghana." *Chains of Fortune: Linking Women Producers and Workers with Global Markets.* Commonwealth Secretariat: London, p. 24.

83 **professional development**   Doherty, B. and Tranchell, S. (2005). "New thinking in international trade? A case study of the Day Chocolate Company." *Sustainable Development,* Volume 13, pp. 166–176.

83 **bananas, mangoes, pineapples**   AgroFair. "AgroFair," available at http: //www.fairtradefruit.com.

83 **Oké U.S.A. was launched**   Rosenthal, J. (2006). Personal communication, 25 April.

83 **Much like Day Chocolate**   AgroFair. "AgroFair," available at http: //www.fairtradefruit.com.

83 **With AgroFair we get a fair price**   AgroFair. "AgroFair," available at http: //www.fairtradefruit.com.

84 **the creation of new trading structures**   Tiffen, P. (2006). Interview with Jacqueline DeCarlo, 20 April.

84 **We dreamed big**   Tiffen, P. (2006). Personal communication, 24 May.

84 **a "gold standard' of Fair Trade**   Twin. *Twin Annual Report 01/02,* available at http: //www. twin.org.uk/downloads/Twin_ Annual_ Report_0102.pdf, p. 2.

84 **My job is to hook them**   Larson, L. (2006). Interview with Jacqueline DeCarlo, 24 March.

84 **supremely delicious coffee**   Larry's Beans. "Larry's Beans," available at http: //www.larrysbeans.com.

85 **just selling great tasting coffee**   Larson, L. (2006). Interview with Jacqueline DeCarlo, 24 March.

85 **occasional whoops of support**   Larry's Beans (2005). "The 'Veggie Bus,' Fueled Entirely by Used Vegetable Oil from Local Restaurants," available at http: //larrysbeans.com/media/press_center/ in_the_news.htm#6.

85 **I'm happy to fuel your journey**   Larson, L. (2006). Interview with Jacqueline DeCarlo, 24 March.

86 **Box:Larry's suggestions to vote with your dollars**   Larson, L. "Larry's Beans" business card. Self-published.

86 **tries to meet people where they are**   Daniels, K. (2006). Interview with Jacqueline DeCarlo, 17 March.

86 **Salvadoran coffee some twenty**   Petchers, S. (2006). Interview with Jacqueline DeCarlo, 24 March.

86 **the first British Fair Trade**   Low, W. and Davenport, E. (2005). "Postcards from the edge: maintaining the alternative character of fair trade." *Sustainable Development,* Volume 13, pp. 143–153.

87 **millions of small farmers**   Petchers, S. (2006). Interview with Jacqueline DeCarlo, 24 March.

87 **Seth Petchers, coffee program director**   Clark, M. (2001). "Fair Trade Ensures a Better Cup of Joe," *Oberlin Alumni Magazine,* Spring, available at http: //www.oberlin.edu/alummag/oamcurrent/ oam_ spring01/profile4.html.

87 **"Yes, we can"**   Petchers, S. (2006). "Coffee Farmers Determination Inspires Action," available at http: //www.oxfamamerica.org/ whatwedo/campaigns/coffee/news_publications/news_update. 2006–04–21.0501142192.

87 **"Talk about us"** Harris, S. (2006). Interview with Jacqueline De-Carlo, 16 March.

88 **a vast number of personal contacts** Gladwell, M. (2000). *The Tipping Point: How Little Things Can Make a Big Difference.* Little, Brown and Company: New York.

88 **environmental justice around the world** Global Exchange. "Global Exchange," available at http://www.globalexchange.org.

89 **an endless pool of people** Sheerin, S. (2006). Interview with Jacqueline DeCarlo, 12 February.

89 **economic conditions of its members** COSURCA (2005). "Aerial fumigations of illicit crops: a case study." 13 September.

89 **the jungle and natural resources** TransFair USA. "TransFair USA', available at http://www.transfairusa.org/content/about/aboutus.php.

89 **a war that has lasted forty years** Lutheran World Relief (2005). *Eradicating Hope in Colombia: Fair Trade, Organic Coffee Farms Damaged by "Plan Colombia" Herbicide Spraying.* Lutheran World Relief: Baltimore, MD.

89 **creating a composting program** TransFair USA. "TransFair USA," available at http://www.transfairusa.org/content/about/aboutus.php.

90 **dropped white clouds of herbicide** Lutheran World Relief (2005). *Eradicating Hope in Colombia: Fair Trade, Organic Coffee Farms Damaged by "Plan Colombia" Herbicide Spraying.* Lutheran World Relief: Baltimore, MD.

Chapter Eight

91 **to improve their practices** Sheehey, E.J. (2006). Personal communication, 13 May.

92 **characterize today's global market** Schumacher, E. F. (1999). *Small Is Beautiful: Economics as if People Mattered.* Hartley & Marks: Point Roberts, WA, p. 199.

92 **protect health and the environment** Wise, T. (2003). "NAFTA's untold stories: Mexico's grassroots response to North American integration" in *Confronting Globalization: Economic Integration and Popular Resistance in Mexico.* T.A. Wise, H. Salazar and L. Carlsen, eds. Kamarian Press: Silver City, NM, p. 5.

92 **easier mechanisms for foreign investment** Selvaggio, K. (2005). "Trade and poverty: what is the relation?" *Social Ministry Gathering*. Catholic Relief Services Conference. 21 February.

92 **"keeping people poor"** Daniels, K. (2006). Interview with Jacqueline DeCarlo, 17 March.

92 **those enslaved because of debts** Jubilee USA Network. "Drop the Debt," available at http: //www.jubileeusa.org.

93 **Group of Eight Industrialized Countries** International Monetary Fund (2006). "The multilateral debt relief initiative." Fact sheet.

93 **unjust and unpayable debts** Jubilee USA Network. "Drop the Debt', available at http: //www. jubileeusa.org.

93 **confront the complex problems** Lafontant, S. (2006). Interview with Jacqueline DeCarlo, 17 March.

93 **$10 million each minute** Selvaggio, K. (2005). "Trade and poverty: what is the relation?" *Social Ministry Gathering*. Catholic Relief Services Conference. 21 February.

93 **The WTO's bias** Oxfam International (2002). *Rigged Rules and Double Standards: Trade, Globalization, and the Fight Against Poverty.* Oxfam International, p. 4.

94 **global rules of trade between nations** World Trade Organization. "What is the WTO?," available at http: //www.wto. org/ english/thewto_e/whatis_e/whatis_e.htm.

94 **In Seattle** Leclair, M.S. (2002). "Fighting the tide: alternative trade organizations in the era of global free trade." *World Development*, Volume 30, p. 949.

94 **trade ministers from African countries** Denny, C. and Elliott, L. (2003). "The WTO in Trade," *The Guardian in association with Action Aid*, 8 September, p. 12.

94 **important roles to play** World Trade Organization. "Ministerial Declaration," available at http://www.wto.org/english/thewto_e/ minist_e/min01_e/mindecl_e.htm.

94 **almost round-the-clock proceedings** Selvaggio, K. (2005). "Trade and poverty: what is the relation?' *Social Ministry Gathering*. Catholic Relief Services Conference. 21 February.

95 **people and the environment** Trade Justice Movement. "Trade Justice Movement," available at http://www.tjm.org.uk.

95 **Box: Excerpts from open letter to governments** *Fair Trade Fair and Sustainable Trade Symposium Proceedings* (2003). Fair Trade

Fair and Sustainable Trade Symposium. Institute for Agriculture and Trade Policy, Comercio Justo Mexico, Equiterre Canada, Oxfam International, and Gerster Consulting: Cancun, Mexico, pp. 28–29.

95 **the Cancun negotiations** Wallach, L. (1999). *The Public Citizen's Pocket Trade Lawyer: The Alphabet Soup of Globalization.* Public Citizen's Global Trade Watch: Washington, DC.

96 **with its liberalization agenda** Daniels, K. (2006). Interview with Jacqueline DeCarlo, 17 March.

96 **economies to compete with the United States** Daniels, K. (2006). Interview with Jacqueline DeCarlo, 17 March.

97 **the proposed FTAA** James, D. (2005). "A Decade's Struggle Ends in Victory," available at http: //www.globalexchange.org/ campaigns/ftaa/3070.html, 15 May.

97 **conventional international trade** International Fair Trade Association. "IFAT Code of Practice," available at http: //www.ifat.org/downloads/monitoringdownloads.shtml.

98 **healthy, nutritious and fairly priced cheese** Family Farm Defenders. "Mission and History," available at http: //www.familyfarmdefenders.org/pmwiki.php/Main/MissionAndHistory.

98 **watermelons in the Northeast** Fair Trade Federation and Fair Trade Resource Network (2005). *Fair Trade Futures: Living a Fair Trade Life Action Guide.* Report. Fair Trade Federation and Fair Trade Resource Network: Washington, DC, p. 13.

98 **just makes common sense** Peck, J. (2005). "Domestic and international fair trade, local food, and sustainable food systems: making the links and expanding the base." Conference presentation. *Fair Trade Futures.* Chicago. 1 October.

Chapter Nine

99 **political, social, and cultural realms** Moen, D.G. (1998). "Analysis of social transformative movements in advanced capitalism: a neo-Gramscian approach." *Journal of Policy and Culture*, Volume 3, available at http: //www.dgmoen.net/essays/ essay_ 4.html.

99 **social justice and change** Fair Trade Futures Conference Planning Council (2005). "Fair Trade Futures Conference Participation Statement." *Fair Trade Futures.* Chicago. 30 September–2 October.

100 **Fair Trade can be confusing** Orth, V. (2006). Fair Trade Futures interview with Jacqueline DeCarlo, April.

100 **July of 2005** United Nations Development Programme (2005). *E-Commerce For Development Report: The Case For Nepalese Artisan Exporters*. United Nations: New York, p. 5.

101 **artisan receives most of the value** Salcedo, D. (2006). Interview with Jacqueline DeCarlo, 14 April.

101 **a "softer face"** Salcedo, D. (2006). "The role of infomediaries in the future of Fair Trade." Conference presentation. *United Students for Fair Trade Convergence*. Denver, CO. 17 February, p. 1.

102 **a relatively inexperienced group** United Nations Development Programme (2005). *E-Commerce For Development Report: The Case For Nepalese Artisan Exporters*. United Nations: New York, p. 5.

102 **overall literacy rate for women in Nepal** Bread for the World Institute (2006). *Frontline Issues in Nutrition Assistance: Hunger Report 2006*. Bread for the World Institute: Washington, DC, p. 163.

102 **take advantage of systems** Salcedo, D. (2006). Interview with Jacqueline DeCarlo, 14 April.

103 **infrastructure and health projects** World of Good. "World of Good," available at http://www.worldofgood.com.

103 **thousands of Fair Trade artisans** Haji, P. (2006). Interview with Jacqueline DeCarlo, 20 March.

103 **Fair Trade craft product** Harbour, H. (2006). "Fair Trade Wage Guide: An Artisan Wage Calculation Tool," available at http://www.fairtradecalculator.net/ calculator.php, p. 1.

104 **increasing their wage per piece** World of Good Development Organization. "Fair Trade Wage Guide," available at http://www.fairtradecalculator.net/index.php.

104 **eighty percent of the product** Rosenthal, J. (2006). Personal communication, 25 April.

105 **a dream come true** Harbour, H. (2006). Personal communication, 30 May.

105 **with teeth** Conroy, M.E. (2005). *Certification Systems as Tools for Natural Asset Building: Potential, Experience to Date, and Critical Challenges 2005*. Political Economy Research Institute, University of Massachusetts Amherst: Amherst, MA, p. 2.

105 **the Fairtrade labeling schemes** Krier, J.-M. (2005). Fair Trade in Europe 2005: Facts and Figures on Fair Trade in 25 European Countries. Fair Trade Advocacy Office: Brussels, p. 7.

106 **people and/or the environment**   Krier, J.-M. (2005). *Fair Trade in Europe 2005: Facts and Figures on Fair Trade in 25 European Countries.* Fair Trade Advocacy Office: Brussels, p. 33.

107 **the commitment to advance payments**   Backe, B. (2006). Interview with Jacqueline DeCarlo, 2 May.

107 **for the foundation of FLO-Cert**   Fairtrade Labeling Organizations International. "FLO International," available at http: //www.fairtrade.net.

108 **total quality of life**   *Declaracion de la iniciativa lationoamerciana y del caribe de pequenos productores de comerico justo.* (2006). J. DeCarlo, trans. Tuxtla Gutierrez, Chiapas, Mexico. 26 March, p. 3.

108 **a new model of trade with justice**   *Declaracion de la iniciativa lationoamerciana y del caribe de pequenos productores de comerico justo.* (2006). J. DeCarlo, trans. Tuxtla Gutierrez, Chiapas, Mexico. 26 March, p. 3.

108 **We shouldn't be an exclusive movement**   Cordon, I. (2005). Fair Trade Futures interview with Shayna Harris, April.

109 **the peoples and the planet**   Arruda, M. (2005). "Solidarity socioeconomy as an integral new system: global vision." Conference presentation. *Workshop on Solidarity Socioeconomy.* Dakar, Senegal. November, p. 1.

109 **extending the scope of Fair Trade**   Etica-Comecio Solidario (2005). *Catalog.* Recife, Brazil. September, p. 3.

109 **Ecuador and Kenya**   Wills, C. (2006). "Fair trade: what's it all about?" *Business Unusual: Successes and Challenges of Fair Trade.* Fair Trade Media: Newcastle-upon-Tyne, UK.

109 **One of the "Seven Sins"**   Argaw, A. and Harris, S. (2006). "All in the same boat'. Keynote address. *United Students for Fair Trade Convergence.* Denver, CO. 17–19 February.

110 **domestic Fair Trade products**   Ericson, R.B. (2006). *The Conscious Consumer: Promoting Economic Justice through Fair Trade.* Fair Trade Resource Network: Washington, DC, p. 33.

Chapter Ten

112 **relationship to money**   Dominquez, J. and Robin, V. (1999). *Your Money Or Your Life: Transforming Your Relationship with Money and Achieving Financial Independence.* Penguin Books: New York.

113 **average U.S. household** Ericson, R.B. (2006). *The Conscious Consumer: Promoting Economic Justice through Fair Trade.* Fair Trade Resource Network: Washington, DC.

115 **Fair Trade Alliance** Co-op America. "Co-op America," available at http://www.coopamerica.org.

115 **stellar example** Gorman, E. (2006). Interview with Jacqueline DeCarlo, 16 March.

116 **food products for their lunchroom** Fair Trade Federation and Fair Trade Resource Network (2005). *Fair Trade Futures: Living a Fair Trade Life Action Guide.* Report. Fair Trade Federation and Fair Trade Resource Network: Washington, DC, p. 9.

116 **Fair Trade activism** Curnow, J. (2006). Interview with Jacqueline DeCarlo, 26 April.

117 **not just about pushing product** Curnow, J. (2006). Interview with Jacqueline DeCarlo, 26 April.

117 **utilizes an affiliate structure** United Students for Fair Trade. "Affiliates: The Grass Roots," available at http://usft.org/index.php?p=/Affiliate.

117 **campuses large and small** United Students for Fair Trade. "United Students for Fair Trade," available at http://www.usft.org.

119 **key force in 2003** Global Exchange. "Advocacy Groups Persuade Procter & Gamble to Offer Fair Trade Certified Coffee," available at http://www.globalexchange.org/campaigns/fairtrade/coffee/ Millstonevictory.html, accessed 1 April 2005.

120 **I.F.T.I. director** Ford, S. (2006). Interview with Jacqueline DeCarlo, March.

120 **Fair Trade Network** Avrill, D. (2005). Interview of member of Saint Therese Parish with Catholic Relief Services, June.

120 **186 Fairtrade towns** Crowther, B. (2006). Personal communication, 6 April.

120 **public meeting in April 2000** Crowther, B. (2005). "Fairtrade towns supporting the FAIRTRADE mark in the U.K.." Conference presentation. *Fair Trade Futures.* Chicago. 1 October.

121 **goals that are evaluated** Fairtrade Foundation. "Fairtrade Town Application Form," available at http://www.fairtrade.org.uk/get_ involved_fairtrade_towns.htm.

121 **Fair Trade coalitions** Burton, G., ed. (2006). National conference call minutes. *Fair Trade Towns.* 1 March.

121 **towns are so appealing** Easson, K. (2005). Fair Trade Futures interview with Jacqueline DeCarlo, 26 April.

122 **start one herself** McGrath, N. (2006). Interview with Jacqueline DeCarlo, 30 March.

123 **front line of consumer education** Grimes, K. (2005). *A Retailer's Guide: Creating a Successful Fair Trade Business.* Fair Trade Resource Network: Washington, DC.

124 **300 stores exclusively devoted** Grimes, K. (2005). *A Retailer's Guide: Creating a Successful Fair Trade Business.* Fair Trade Resource Network: Washington, DC.

Glossary

advocacy The support of a particular cause to sway public policy or general philosophy of a group.

capitalism An economic system based on private ownership of goods in which supply and demand in a free market establish prices.

child labor The illegal and/or unethical use of children to produce goods.

consumer The purchaser of a good or service.

cottage industry Micro-industries that usually consist of small groups of workers that supply goods to larger businesses.

debt relief The act of forgiving the funds borrowed by a person, organization, or government.

equal exchange A Massachusetts-based organization that distributes various foods produced by farmer cooperatives in Latin America, Africa and Asia.

European Union An economic cooperative of 27 member states that collaborates on economic policies related to their regions.

fair trade An economic model that helps producers in developing countries more competitively offer their goods to the global economy.

free markets Markets that are uninhibited by governmental control that allow for competition of goods and services.

free trade An economic system that allows people to trade goods and services freely without the hindrance of government.

International Monetary Fund The international organization that oversees the economic stability of the world's major economies.

middleman A person who facilitates an economic transaction between two parties.

multinational corporation A corporation that operates in more than one nation.

networking The act of making business connections and relationships.

sustainability The environmental friendliness of something such as a means of production.

sweat-free community Places where sweatshops have been eliminated.

sweatshops Factories in which the workers have little power to demand higher wages or humane working conditions.

transparency The act of making corporate or financial information free for public viewing and scrutiny.

wage Money earned from labor.

World Trade Organization The organization that oversees and monitors trade between nations.

For more information

Fair Trade Federation
1718 M Street NW #381
Washington DC 20036
(202) 636-3547
Web site: http://www.fairtradefederation.org
This association was formed in 1996 "to bring Fair Trade wholesalers, retailers and producers together to share information on their Fair Trade work and collaborate on how to bring awareness of Fair Trade to the U.S. market." Fair Trade Federation membership consists of some 230 businesses and non-governmental organizations committed to selling only Fair Trade products.

Fairtrade Labeling Organizations International
Bonner Talweg 177
53129 Bonn, Germany
+49 228 949230
Web site: http://www.fairtrade.net
This is one of the biggest international social economic certification bodies worldwide. According to its Web site, F.L.O. regularly inspects and certifies about 420 producer organisations in 50 countries in Africa, Asia and Latin America.

Interfaith Fair Trade Initiative of Lutheran World Relief
700 Light Street
Baltimore, MD 21230
(410) 230-2800
Web site: http://www.lwr.org
This initiative coordinates U.S. based faith groups active in Fair Trade, including American Friends Service Committee, American Jewish World Service, Catholic Relief Services, Church of the Brethren, Episcopal Relief and Development, Jewish Fund for Justice, Lutheran

World Relief, Mennonite Central Committee, Presbyterian Church (U.S.A.), Religious Action Center, Reform Judaism, Unitarian Universalist Service Committee, United Church of Christ, and United Methodist Committee on Relief.

International Finance Corporation
2121 Pennsylvania Avenue NW
Washington, DC 20433 USA
(202) 473-1000
Web site: http://www.ifc.org
A member of the World Bank Group, the IFC describes itself as a global investor and advisor committed to promoting sustainable projects in developing countries that are economically beneficial, financially and commercially sound, and environmentally and socially sustainable.

United Nations
Millennium Campaign
304 East 45th Street, FF-612
New York, NY 10017
(212) 906-6242
Web site: http://www.EndPoverty2015.org
The Millennuim Campaign is a United Nations–led effort to support "citizens' efforts to hold their government to account for the Millennium promise," as discussed in chapter one. Because it is funded by the United Nations, which is funded by member nations, this particular campaign features softtouch tactics, such as promoting the World Food Program's "Walk the World," a public relations effort to encourage people to participate in marches against child hunger.

World Trade Organization
Centre William Rappard
Rue de Lausanne 154
CH-1211 Geneva 21, Switzerland
+41 (0)22 739 51 11
Web site: http://www.wto.org
The WTO deals with the rules of trade between nations. WTO agreements are, as explained by the organization's Web site, negotiated and

signed by the bulk of the world's trading nations and ratified in their parliaments. The goal is to help producers of goods and services, exporters, and importers conduct their business.

Web Sites

Due to the changing nature of Internet links, Rosen Publishing has developed an online list of Web sites related to the subject of this book. This site is updated regularly. Please use this link to access the list:

Web site: http://www.rosenlinks.com/ciss/fair

For further reading

Grimes, Kimberly, and B. Lynne Milgram, eds. *Artisans and Cooperatives: Developing Alternative Trade for the Global Economy.* Tucson, AZ: University of Arizona Press, 2000.

Krier, Jean-Marie. *Fair Trade in Europe 2005: Facts and Figures on Fair Trade in 25 European Countries.* Brussels, Germany: Fair Trade Advocacy Office, 2005.

Littrell, Mary, and Marsha Dickson. *Social Responsibility in the Global Market: Fair Trade of Cultural Products.* Thousand Oaks, CA: Sage Publications, 1999.

Nicholls, Alex, and Charlotte Opal. *Fair Trade: Market-Driven Ethical Consumption.* Thousand Oaks, CA: Sage Publications, 2005.

Oxfam International. *Rigged Rules and Double Standards: Trade, Globalization, and the Fight Against Poverty.* Boston, MA: Oxfam International, 2002.

Redfern, Andy, and Paul Snedker. *Creating Market Opportunities for Small Enterprises: Experiences of the Fair Trade Movement.* Geneva, Switzerland: International Labour Organization, 2002.

United for a Fair Economy. *Free Trade Area of the Americas for Beginners.* Boston, MA: United for a Fair Economy, 2004.

Index

About the Author

Jacqueline DeCarlo is Fair Trade program advisor of Catholic Relief Services, and former director of the Fair Trade Resource Network.